A BRIEF INTRODUTION TO

THE ARABIC ALPHABET:
ITS ORIGINS AND VARIOUS FORMS

BRIEF INTRODUCTIONS SERIES

Modern Arabic Literature

Astronomy in the Middle East

A BRIEF INTRODUCTION TO

THE ARABIC ALPHABET:
ITS ORIGINS AND VARIOUS FORMS

JOHN F. HEALEY AND G. REX SMITH

SAQI

London San Francisco Beirut

ISBN: 978-0-86356-431-4

First published by Saqi, 2009

A full CIP record for this book is available from the British Library.

A full CIP record for this book is available from the Library of Congress.

Manufactured in Lebanon

SAQI

26 Westbourne Grove, London W2 5RH
825 Page Street, Suite 203, Berkeley, California 94710
Tabet Building, Mneimneh Street, Hamra, Beirut
www.saqibooks.com

Contents

Illustrations

Note on Transliteration

When transliterating words into English, special signs and diacritics (mostly dots) are normally used where there is no English equivalent to the letter in question: ' ḥ ṭ ' ṣ š (= *sh*, which is generally preferred in transliterating Arabic), etc. Where necessary vowels are represented as short (*a e i o u*) and long (*ā ē ī ō ū*). When an individual letter appears in discussion in italic (e.g. *b*), the reference is normally to its written form; when the sound represented is being referred to double slashes enclose it: /b/.

Introduction

This book has the modest ambition of presenting an easily accessible account of the origins and history of the Arabic script. While there are numerous accounts of writing systems, we are not aware of any account of this precise scope aimed at university undergraduates and the general reader. This Introduction is mainly concerned with discussion of some of the technicalities of the development of scripts and the religious significance attached to writing by the peoples of the Middle East.

Writing and Language

It is necessary to begin by drawing attention to the difference between writing and language. Human languages are natural phenomena which have developed over millennia. Language consists of a set of sounds deployed in a meaningful pattern. There were millennia before the invention of writing during which languages existed but were never written down. We can be sure that many languages developed and subsequently became extinct during this time. There are still today languages in some parts of the world which have never been written down, especially in South America and southern Asia.

The fact that language and script are two separate things is illustrated by the way that occasionally a decision is made, usually by a state, to change its writing system. The best example in the Middle Eastern context is that of Turkey. In the Ottoman period Turkish was written using an adapted form of the Arabic script. Under the Turkish Republic, in 1928, Atatürk decided to switch to the so-called Latin script, the script used for the main European languages like English. A few extra signs were adopted to represent sounds common in Turkish but not represented in the Latin script. Thus ç for the sound /ch/ as in "church" and ş for /sh/ as in "shop". (There are some less obvious adaptations: Turkish c stands for /j/ as in "jam", while Turkish j stands for the sound in the middle of the word "treasure".)

In principle any language can be written down in any writing system and a change of writing system has no direct bearing on the way a language sounds, though the fact that a language is written down does tend to create a conservative force which encourages continuity and slows the rate of change. The classical Arabic of the Quran came to be regarded as Arabic *par excellence* with a divine sanction and was a model for all later literature.

Writing Systems

Before we consider the historical origins of writing systems (i.e. scripts), it is worth noting that writing systems are highly artificial creations of the relatively recent past: there was no true writing at all before the middle of the fourth millennium BCE.

The only limit on the devising of writing systems is the limit of the human imagination, though in fact there is a basic typology of writing systems, since most fall into a limited number of types. Those which concern us at the beginning of this story are syllabic systems and alphabetic systems.

It is clear that writing began in the Middle Eastern world in association with the great civilizations of Egypt and Mesopotamia in the late fourth millennium BCE, perhaps around 3300 BCE. Which of the two can claim the priority is not entirely clear, though most scholars in the field think that Mesopotamia was earlier, with writings on clay from Uruk c. 3300 BCE. Egypt followed c. 3100 BCE. Both systems were syllabic, i.e. signs were devised to represent syllables, units of sound consisting normally of a consonantal sound or sounds and a vocalic sound. Thus in a word like "consonantal" the word would be broken down into syllables as *con-son-ant-al* and four signs would be used to represent these four syllables. The same sign as the one used for *al* could also be used in writing the word *al-pha-bet*. The actual signs used for the syllables had an origin as pictographs, pictures of things turned into formalized symbols. A picture of an ant might represent the syllable *ant* in *con-son-ant-al*. The picture then gradually ceased to be a pictograph and came to stand for a syllable. The same idea is seen in the rebus-type puzzles which use this principle.

Of course it was for Ancient Egyptian and the ancient languages of Mesopotamia (Sumerian and Akkadian) that the syllabic signs were used, not English! One consequence of this is the fact that certain sounds had to be accounted for which do not exist in English (or other European languages). Signs had to be devised to represent the sounds of each language: when one writing system was adapted for use by another language, there were often weaknesses in the system and minor changes were made. We will see much later that this same process of adaptation of one script to the needs of a different language can result, for example, in the addition of dots (called diacritics) to indicate sounds that would otherwise remain unrepresented.

If the reader of this cares to try the exercise of dividing a whole paragraph of English text into syllables, he or she will soon see that there is a very large number of different syllables in English, as there is also in languages like Akkadian. The consequence of this is that the systems which emerged for syllabic writing had extremely large numbers of signs. The total number of signs in the Akkadian syllabary is about 500, though not all of them were in use at any one time. But to be a reasonably competent reader or writer of Akkadian one would need to be able to recognize and deploy several hundred signs. Hence the scribal profession involved years of training and was restricted to specialists.

The second system, which developed in the Middle East in the second millennium (i.e. between 2000 and 1000 BCE), was alphabetical, though not quite alphabetical in our modern sense. This newer system built on the idea that instead of representing a syllable by a single sign one could devise a set of signs which represented each separate sound. In principle this involved separating all the consonants and vowels into individual bits of the language. Thus our sample words above, "consonantal" and "alphabet", would now be written *c-o-n-s-o-n-a-n-t-a-l* (in which the same sign for *n* recurs three times and the sign for *a* occurs twice) and *a-l-p-h-a-b-e-t* (in which the signs for *a*, *l* and *t* which occur in "consonantal" appear again). With an alphabetic script the number of signs needed is much smaller: English has 26, Hebrew and Syriac have 22, Arabic has 28.

This newly invented alphabetic writing system was, however, different from our modern system in that only the consonants were represented. The vowels were supplied by the reader of the text, who normally knew the language in question and did not have too much difficulty reading the consonantal text. This is clear today from the fact that the Hebrew and Arabic alphabets are still largely consonantal and newspapers in these languages, for example, are printed largely without vowel indicators. (It is not even all that difficult in English: *th ct st n th mt*, and this kind of abbreviated spelling has recently become popular in text-messaging.)

Direction of Writing

Another issue which introduces variability in writing systems is the question of the direction of writing. The direction is purely conventional. Hebrew and Arabic are written from right to left, but Akkadian and another language closely related to Hebrew, Ugaritic, are written from left to right. Vertical writing was also quite common in antiquity and most extraordinary of all from a modern perspective is the *boustrophedon* writing found in early Greek inscriptions and in the pre-Islamic inscriptions of ancient Yemen. "Boustrophedon" means "(like) an ox ploughing" and the writing in question changes direction in alternate lines (a rather efficient system, since it would be inefficient to take your ox back to the beginning of the first furrow before cutting the second).

As we will see, alphabetic writing in the Middle East settled down almost universally to the right-to-left direction. When the alphabet was borrowed from the Middle East by the Greeks they wrote it from left to right: hence our European languages' preference for left to right.

Diversification of Writing Styles

Writing systems, like languages, have a natural tendency to diversify, especially in isolation from each other. Just as in the case of languages isolated regional dialects can, in the long run, become mutually unintelligible, so also with writing styles. It is quite difficult for a modern British reader of English to decipher some styles of handwriting which were used in the nineteenth century. In German there are even greater extremes, with the nineteenth-century chancery hand ("hand" here means "handwriting style") almost completely illegible to a modern German.

When the alphabetic writing system became universal in the western part of the Middle East towards the end of the second millennium BCE, its development did not then cease. Gradually regional varieties of the alphabet emerged. At first they were mutually intelligible: an Aramaean scribe could read the letters of a Moabite inscription (though not necessarily understand the language very well), just as we can read aloud Latin inscriptions even if we do not know any Latin. Eventually, however, the differences in the different scribal schools or traditions became so large that we can speak in terms of different scripts, so that it is almost certain that in the first century CE Judaeans and Nabataeans, near neighbours on each side of the River Jordan using alphabets with a common ancestor, would not have been able to read each other's writing.

Another aspect of diversification is particularly important in the study of the origins of the Arabic script. This arises from the fact that we use different forms of script for different purposes. What you are reading now bears little similarity to the style of script you use in writing birthday cards or shopping lists.

For a start, printed English typefaces like the one you are reading make no provision for the joining of letters. In handwriting most of us join most of the letters most of the time. This feature of "joined-up writing" or "ligatured script" is a relatively late phenomenon in the history of ancient Near Eastern scripts. The early forms of the alphabet, used for example for Phoenician and Hebrew, used only isolated forms of the individual letters.

An early move away from this simple position involved the creation of "final" forms of letters. This is familiar to us in handwritten English, where it is common to add a final flourish to the final letter of a word, but it became a fixed convention in the early alphabetic scripts; special final forms of certain letters were always used when the letter came at the end of the word.

There is another point to be noted here. Early forms of the alphabetic scripts did not always separate words. We use a space to separate words, but the earliest efforts at separating words employed dots or vertical lines for this purpose. One can see that the use of final forms of letters was advantageous in such circumstances, since the use of the final form would indicate that the word was finished. The convention of using capital letters at the *beginning* of a sentence in English and at the beginning of nouns in German is relatively modern and none of the Middle Eastern scripts has capital letters at all.

Gradually the habit of linking letters developed. At first the method of making the linkages was arbitrary and purely instinctive, though conventions soon established themselves, such that the joins had to be made in a particular way. Thus in scripts such as the Arabic script and the Syriac script letters within words are normally joined together (though there are some linkages which are ruled out) and these joins have to be made in a particular way. If one can imagine an analogy with English, it is perfectly normal in handwriting to make linking lines between the *a*, *n* and *d* in the word "and", but it would be eccentric in the extreme to make the links between the tops of the letters! In scripts like Arabic and Syriac the rules on how to make the links are rigid and not a matter of personal preference.

In English (as also in many other languages) there is another major writing style commonly in use, a monumental script, normally capital letters, which is used for such public purposes as writing inscriptions on buildings and registration numbers on cars. The Middle Eastern scripts like the Hebrew and Arabic scripts do not have capital letters, but they do have "monumental" forms of script used for public purposes. Only a specialist calligrapher would attempt to use these more elaborate forms of script in writing on paper (or in ancient times on parchment or papyrus). Instead, a flowing, often simplified form of script is used for everyday purposes, a "cursive" script. In the end the monumental and cursive forms of script can differ considerably and reading the cursive handwriting of modern Arabic, for example, presents a challenge even to the competent Arabist.

Calligraphy is essentially the beautification of writing so that it becomes a work of art in itself and all the ancient and modern script traditions know this phenomenon. Inscriptions and (usually religious) manuscripts are designed to look impressive even before the content of the writing is considered. Despite the fact that the alphabet was much easier to learn than the syllabic writing systems, it seems that literacy was still far from universal. Decorative writing on a building or in a large scroll or codex (book) could have an impact on such illiterates, just as the stained-glass windows in medieval cathedrals told the story of salvation to the peasantry. In the Islamic tradition calligraphy came to be regarded as one of the highest art-forms, entirely compatible with the Islamic reluctance to paint pictures especially of sacred realities.

A Note on Languages

Despite the fact that language and writing are quite separate things (above), it is, of course, historically inevitable that particular writing systems have come to be associated with particular languages and cultures.

The syllabic system used for Sumerian and Akkadian is closely associated with both, and also with Hittite and other ancient Near Eastern languages, despite the fact that Sumerian, Akkadian and Hittite are linguistically unrelated to each other. In other words the script, often called "cuneiform" because its syllabic signs consist of wedge-shaped marks in different combinations (Latin *cuneus* = "wedge"), became a cultural artefact which could be used across language barriers. In a similar way the Arabic script was adapted for use for Turkish and Persian (and other Islamic languages) as part of the spread of Arab-Islamic culture.

The main languages of the Middle East which are involved in the early history of the alphabet belong to the Semitic language group, which includes, apart from Arabic and Hebrew, such languages as Aramaic and Syriac, Phoenician and Moabite, Sabaic and related languages in south Arabia (Yemen) and the languages of Ethiopia. There are also some ancient Semitic languages for which cuneiform or an adapted alphabetic cuneiform were used (Akkadian and Ugaritic respectively). The term "Semitic" for these languages derives from an eighteenth-century European interpretation of the Hebrew Bible, which has Shem or Sem as the ancestor of the speakers of the languages in question.

The details of the interrelationships of these Semitic languages need not concern us here, but there are some shared features which are worth noting in the context of the history of the alphabet. In all of these languages the functions of vowels are different from the functions of consonants. Consonants tend to convey general meanings of words, connecting them with semantic fields. The vowels have the function of pinning down the precise meaning. A good analogy in English is provided by the words "sing", "sang", "sung" and "song". From this set of words one could conclude that the basic idea of singing is represented by "s-ng" and the various actual meanings are distinguished by the vowels. This principle is ubiquitous in the Semitic languages. To take an Arabic example, the set of "root" consonants *ktb* has to do fundamentally with writing: *kataba* means "he wrote", *kitāb* means "book", *kutub* means "books", *kātib* means "scribe", etc. One can see, therefore, that the vowels have a different function from the consonants.

This fact is connected with the way that a consonant-only alphabet was adopted in the first place (above). The problem with such an alphabet lies in its ambiguity, acutely felt by a learner of the language or a non-native speaker or when a previously unknown word is suddenly introduced into the text. It is because of this fundamental ambiguity in the scripts that modifications were gradually introduced, for Arabic, Hebrew and Syriac, for example, designed to supply vowel-indicators and resolve the ambiguity. Undoubtedly a major motive here was religious: if your sacred scripture, the word of God, was written down in an ambiguous writing system, it might be misread in public or in private and this could potentially lead to doctrinal error or even scandal.

The Human Significance of Writing

Before launching into our history of the antecedents of the Arabic alphabet, it is worth reflecting on the importance of writing in the world of the ancient Near East, including its religious importance.

The devising of writing in the fourth millennium BCE was, it appears, prompted by the practical needs arising in the lives of the inhabitants of complex urban societies. If you live all your life in a self-sufficient village, you may have little need for writing, but as villages began to interact and focus on bigger urban centres, with markets, specialized craftsmen, temples and rulers (both of which soon demanded taxes), it became essential to develop recording systems to keep track of complex transactions. Although such complexity existed in earlier times too, in the fourth millennium BCE there was a step change in the level of complexity associated with urbanization.

Once invented, writing spread. Soon it began to be used for higher purposes, writing letters, recording lists of property, listings of kings and eventually telling stories and recording laws. Kings used writing as a tool of their propaganda and to promulgate their laws. The most iconic inscribed artefacts in antiquity include the Laws of Hammurabi and the Rosetta Stone.

In due course, in the third and second millennia BCE, literature in something like our modern sense emerged, with moving epics like the *Epic of Gilgamesh* in Akkadian and the Baal mythology of ancient Ugarit. Much has survived from ancient Egypt and Mesopotamia especially and both cultures had a high regard for writing, to such an extent that the introduction of writing was ascribed to one of the gods. In Egypt the god in question was Thoth, interpreted later as identical with Greek Hermes. In Mesopotamia it was Nabu, the scribe god, and the skill of writing was also communicated to the semi-divine Adapa by his father the god Ea. In the Judaeo-Christian tradition the knowledge of writing was communicated to men by Enoch the Scribe (Gen. 5: 21-4). In Greece, in addition to traditions about Hermes, there is a specific report on the arrival of the Greek writing system, which was ascribed to the semi-mythological Kadmos, son of the king of Tyre (Herodotus V, 58). The Greeks are undoubtedly amongst the greatest users of writing in the ancient world, generating the Homeric literature and the works of the great historians and philosophers.

Writing and the Divine

But so far as the Middle East is concerned, there is no doubt that the finest product of the art of writing in the pre-Roman period is the Hebrew Bible. Created over a long period of time, the Hebrew Bible is the only work of its kind to survive, though there must have been other cultures of the first millennium BCE with some similar sacred writings. The case of the Israelites is, however, special in that tremendous importance was attached to the Word of God as represented in the sacred text. There is a profound theology involved here, but what concerns us in this context is the fact that this theology turned the written text into a symbol of divine revelation. In the Jewish tradition this became even more important when the other focus of Judaism, the Jerusalem Temple, was destroyed in 70 CE. Thereafter God's contact with his chosen people depended entirely on the Torah and the other writings of the Hebrew Bible. The study of that deposit of revelation and the traditions accompanying it became the focus of Judaism. The text as transmitted was regarded as sacrosanct, unchangeable and embodying God's will. Some groups, on the basis of this theology, looked for hidden messages and meanings in the Bible, perhaps not intended by the original authors, but intended by the divine hand which guided them. The more esoteric branches of Judaism, such as the Kabbalah, are based on this notion.

In Christianity there was never the same attitude to the letters and words of Scripture and this is reflected in the fact that the

Bible, Old Testament and New, was quickly translated into other languages such as Latin and Syriac for the convenience of the faithful: the theological foundation of the Church rested on the person of Jesus and the authority of bishops rather than the close reading of every word of the Bible. This was, of course, challenged at the time of the European Reformation.

In Islam we find an attitude to the written word of God which is much more like the Jewish attitude. The Quran is literally the word of God: perfect in every respect (including linguistically), unchangeable, indeed, in the view of most Muslims, in some sense eternal. As in Judaism it is, therefore, appropriate to pore over every detail of the text to investigate its meanings, whether they be on the surface or hidden below it. The Quran becomes emblematic of Islam, the physical embodiment on earth of the Heavenly Quran which reflects perfectly the divine will. It is the ever-present Word of God, just as for orthodox Christians the Word of God is really present in the Eucharist. In other words the Quran is a sacrament, the outward sign of a spiritual reality. Hence it is decorated and made beautiful through calligraphy and the calligraphic art comes to have a major role in Islam: the divine and the holy cannot be embellished in pictures and statues, but the words of the Quran take their place and deserve as much artistic effort and respect as is given by Jews to the Torah.

1 - The Alphabet before Islam

The aim in this chapter is to give an account of the origins of the kind of alphabetic writing which led ultimately to the development of the Arabic alphabet.

By 1000 BCE alphabetic writing was beginning to dominate the western regions of the Middle East, especially Syria, the Lebanese coast, Palestine, Jordan and Arabia, though syllabic writing continued in its entrenched position in Egypt and Mesopotamia. The reasons for the rapid advance of the alphabet are unclear, but one factor is probably the decline of cuneiform culture and Egyptian influence in these areas at the end of the second millennium BCE. The process by which this alphabetic writing developed is quite complicated and there were rival alphabetic systems during the late second millennium BCE.

The first evidence of alphabetic writing suggests it was devised under the inspiration of certain aspects of the Egyptian syllabic system. In this system there were signs which stood for single consonantal sounds followed by any vowel. However, so far as we can see it was not these single-consonant signs which were borrowed to form a separate alphabet. The procedure adopted was slightly different and involved a principle which we now call "acrophony". This word is related to the word acronym and it specifically means "systematization based on the initial sound of words". This at first seems rather obscure, but the concept is simple.

Most of the Egyptian syllabic signs consisted originally of small pictures of the thing represented by the sign. The syllable *ra* is also the word for "mouth" in Egyptian; hence the sign to represent this syllable was a small picture of a mouth: ⬭ . Following the acrophonic principle, this sign began to be used also simply to represent the first sound of this word for mouth, /r/. Single-sound signs of this kind were incorporated into the Egyptian writing system, but they were used alongside syllabic signs and the Egyptians did not make the transition to alphabetic writing.

The transition was made when this basic idea was applied by speakers of Semitic dialects to their own language, using some of the originally Egyptian hieroglyphic signs. For example, the word for "house" in West Semitic was *bētu*. The hieroglyph for the equivalent word in Egyptian was a small ground-plan of a house: ⌐⌐ . This sign was adopted by the speakers of the Semitic dialect in question to represent /b/. On the same principle there were devised signs for most of the consonants.

Some of the signs represented consonants which have no simple equivalent in English and these have to be represented in transliteration by the addition of diacritics. Thus *ḫ ṭ ṣ š* (= *sh*) and also the first letter of the alphabet, represented in transliteration as an apostrophe, '. This last sign represents what is called a glottal stop and the word which provided the acrophonic letter of the alphabet is the word written alphabetically as '*lp* ('*alpu*) and meaning "bull". The first letter of this word was inscribed as , which represented the head of a bull. This provides another simple example of acrophony.

The first clear evidence of this kind of alphabetic writing came from small inscriptions produced by people connected with the turquoise mines at Serabit al-Khadim in Sinai and they are therefore often called the Proto-Sinaitic inscriptions. They are not easy to date, but probably come from about 1700-1500 BCE. Unfortunately the inscriptions are very short and enigmatic. E.g. there are short religious dedications saying *lb'lt*, "(dedicated) to (the goddess) Ba'alat". These small inscriptions are sometimes written vertically.

However, it was always intrinsically improbable that the alphabet had actually been devised in Sinai, far away from the scribal schools and cultural centres. Subsequent discoveries in Palestine and an intense interest in devising new writing systems on the Levantine coast both point to an origin of this alphabet in that region.

There were other experiments in alphabetic writing shortly afterwards, though probably inspired by the first devising of the alphabet already described. The best known of these experiments was the Ugaritic alphabet, used mainly at the ancient city of Ugarit on the north Syrian coast. This was a cosmopolitan city in the Late Bronze Age (1500-1200 BCE) and excavations have produced texts in Egyptian, Akkadian, Hurrian and also in the local language, now called Ugaritic.

27

This local language was written in a cuneiform script (made up of wedge-shaped signs), but using an alphabet of 30 letters. It appears that in this area the practice of writing on clay in the cuneiform tradition was deeply entrenched and the scribes decided to create a compromise form of writing: cuneiform signs for alphabetic values. They also retained the left-to-right direction of writing which was used for Mesopotamian cuneiform. Despite a short-lived flourishing, this writing system in fact disappeared when Ugarit was destroyed by the Sea Peoples around 1200 BCE.

It was not the cuneiform version of the alphabet which survived, but the linear form evidenced in the Proto-Sinaitic inscriptions. "Linear" in this context means made up of signs formed by drawing or inscribing lines (not wedges). This linear alphabet begins to appear in small inscriptions from Palestine and Lebanon soon after c. 1200 BCE. As it spread and became popular, this basic alphabet was standardized and stylized. Stylization refers to the process whereby pictures especially are reduced to basic and characteristic outlines (like the small picture of a typical bus painted on a bus-stop or the little man on the door of a public convenience!).

The right-to-left direction of writing, which had initially been optional, became fixed by convention as the newly developed alphabet began to be used in the various city-states of the Levant. This was a period, from c. 1200 BCE, during which a number of independent states were emerging after centuries of Egyptian and Hittite domination. The alphabet filled the need for a writing system suitable for the Semitic languages spoken in these kingdoms. There were the Phoenician cities (gradually coalescing), Israel (and the much less stable and significant Judah), Ammon, Moab and Edom in what is now Jordan, and, of great long-term historical significance, the Aramaean states of Syria (especially Damascus).

The Phoenician cities had a certain cultural primacy here (having already had centuries of contact with Egypt and Mesopotamia) and it was in Phoenicia that the linear alphabet was perfected and standardized by about 1050 BCE. Soon after this date there appear in Phoenicia lengthy inscriptions in the new script, mostly connected with tombs.

It was from the Phoenicians that the alphabet was transmitted to the other kingdoms of the region and also to the Greeks and southern Arabia. Before we look at these individual kingdoms and their use of the alphabet, it is useful to note that there are considerable debates about the precise dates of transmission of the alphabet to each. Since absolute dating is rarely provided in ancient inscriptions from this area, we have to rely to some extent on archaeological evidence and sometimes on palaeography.

Palaeography is concerned with the historical variation in forms of writing. Just as an expert can distinguish English handwriting of the sixteenth century from that of the nineteenth century, so the expert in ancient inscriptions can often make an informed judgement about the date of an inscription by studying how it fits into a whole sequence of dated and non-dated inscriptions. Putting the argument crudely, if there is a peculiar letter-form which only appears after the seventh century BCE, it is probable that a newly discovered undated inscription which contains this letter-form will not be from before the seventh century BCE.

This sometimes has a bearing on the issue of the date of transmission of the alphabet to a particular region. A clear

example is provided by the Semitic consonant called '*ayin* –
it's another of those letters which has no equivalent sound in
English. The original pictograph which was the basis for
determining the shape of this letter was a picture of an eye:
👁. As part of the process of stylization of this letter, the
oval shape was gradually rounded (⊙), then, when the
connection with eyes was forgotten or no longer important,
the dot was omitted. (To take the development of this letter
further into the later period, as we will see later, the circle
began to be written as two strokes almost like brackets: ( )
and then the top was opened up so that it became 𝕝). We
thus have a kind of history of the letter, a palaeographic
sequence. The changes of shape can be approximately dated.

This has a bearing on the date of the transmission of the
alphabet to the Greeks and Aramaeans, since in both cases
there are early inscriptions which use this letter and in which
the dot is still present: this suggests (though there is much
debate) that the alphabet was borrowed by the Greeks and
Aramaeans *before* the dot disappeared: why otherwise would
they introduce the dot? And this in turn implies an early date
of transmission of the alphabet to these peoples. Some would
date it before 1200 BCE.

This is to be considered against the whole background of
standardization and stylization. Another aspect of the
alphabet which was quickly standardized was the alphabetic
order. What became the standard order in the west Semitic
languages (Phoenician, Hebrew, Aramaic, etc.) was: ' *b g d h
w z ḥ ṭ y k l m n s ' p ṣ q r š* (= *sh*) *t*. This alphabetic order is
found in school texts used in the training of scribes as early as
in the Ugaritic material, but it is then reflected, e.g., in the
alphabetic order which is found in the Hebrew Bible (Psalms

25 and 34 begin each line with a successive letter of the alphabet). The Greeks made various adaptations of Semitic letters to suit their own language: we will discuss these briefly later. But the resemblance between this ancient Semitic alphabetic order and the order of the Greek letters can immediately be seen. Greek has *alpha beta gamma delta* .... and English (...K L M N... Q R S T...) uses a variation on this order derived from Latin: A B C D (note that there is no *c* in the Semitic or Greek alphabets).

This alphabetic order prevailed in the Levant and in the West, but c. 1000 BCE other alphabetic orders existed. One which is quite widely attested begins with *h l ḥ m* ... It is known in full usage in south Arabia, but there are sporadic evidences of it from Ugarit and elsewhere in the north. In the end it prevailed only in ancient Yemen and in Ethiopia.

We now turn to comment on the spread of the alphabet to the various places already mentioned. For reasons of linkage with what follows in the next chapter, we will leave the Aramaeans and Aramaic until last.

Israel and Judah

The ancient Israelites – we use this term broadly, though it disguises a host of historical problems about whether the United Kingdom under David and Solomon ever existed as a unitary state – appear to have borrowed the alphabet from the Phoenicians along with much else. The Bible itself tells us that the first Israelites depended for iron-working technology on the Phoenicians and David and Solomon are said to have imported Phoenician craftsmen to build the palace and temple.

31

The earliest inscription which is usually counted as Hebrew is the Gezer Calendar, so-called because it lists agricultural activities throughout the year. It is very short and its writing and language are hard to distinguish from Phoenician (hence the doubt about whether it should be counted as Hebrew), but it was found within what became Israelite territory. It dates to about 900 BCE. Thereafter we have an increasing number of ancient Hebrew inscriptions, notably ostraca (pieces of pottery used for writing practical documents like letters and lists) from Samaria, Lachish and elsewhere. Official inscriptions rarely survive, but a notable exception is the Siloam tunnel inscription now in Istanbul. This was found in a tunnel under Jerusalem and it commemorates the creation of the tunnel probably during the reign of King Hezekiah in c. 700 BCE. Here we have a mature Hebrew script with some calligraphic features (i.e. it was meant to look good!) and it is probable that it was in this sort of script that the earliest parts of the Bible were written down.

The Hebrew script being referred to here is often called Palaeo-Hebrew, to distinguish it from the script which later came to be used for all purposes (including the writing of the Bible) and which is still in use today (though the handwritten form of modern Hebrew diverges quite a lot from the printed script, often called the square script, used in standard printings of the Bible and liturgical books). This later script, which of course came to be called "Hebrew", is in fact a later derivative of the Aramaic script (see more below). It is the script used in the writing of the Dead Sea Scrolls, while the Palaeo-Hebrew script survived in use among the Samaritan sect, where the Torah is preserved in this old script.

The Transjordanian Kingdoms

Alongside the Israelites there were other kingdoms emerging at the same time: the Ammonites in the area east of the Jordan and including modern Amman, the Moabites a little further south, and the Edomites at the southern end of the Dead Sea in the area including Petra. These peoples too adopted the Phoenician alphabet. The only one of the three for which we have substantial evidence is Moabite: a lengthy Moabite inscription, dated to c. 850 BCE, records the victories of a Moabite king, Mesha. The script is clearly derived from the Phoenician, but as in the case of the Palaeo-Hebrew script, it gradually diversified from it, developing its own peculiarities.

The Greeks

We have already alluded to the transmission of the alphabet to the Greeks. The date of this transmission is disputed somewhat, since there is a minority view that the Greeks borrowed the alphabet at a very early stage, perhaps before 1200 BCE when the letter-forms were still developing. One piece of evidence is the fact that in the earliest inscriptions, otherwise undated, some of the letter-forms are very archaic. However, the consensus is that this borrowing took place after 800 BCE and the early inscriptions are assigned to this horizon by experts in Greek epigraphy (writings on stone).

The Greeks at this date did not have a unified state and the alphabet varied in different regions. It seems to have been through trade with Phoenicia that the alphabet was introduced and ancient Greek authors like Herodotus acknowledge the Phoenician role by calling the script "the Phoenician letters" and ascribing the introduction to a legendary figure Kadmos, who supposedly came from Phoenicia. Even without this legend, the Middle Eastern origin of the Greek alphabet would not be in doubt. Firstly, there is the form of the letters: several resemble very closely the Phoenician letters. Secondly, the Greek alphabetic order is clearly influenced by the Semitic order. And thirdly, perhaps the most dramatic evidence, is the fact that the names of most of the Greek letters used by Greeks are obviously derived from a Semitic-language source: the name *alpha* for the first letter comes from '*alpu* (above) and the name of the second, *beta*, comes from *bētu* (above). These words have no meaning in Greek except as the names of the letters.

Although the Greeks borrowed, and standardized in their own way, the forms of the letters, they introduced one major innovation: they decided to use some letters to represent vowels. This was made easier by the fact that there were some letters of the Phoenician alphabet which were not needed for Greek since Greek did not have the corresponding consonant. In an earlier discussion, we referred to the Semitic consonant called '*ayin*, which in the early period came to be written as a circle. This consonant existed in the West Semitic languages, as it does also in Arabic (ع), but there is no such sound in Greek (or other European languages). Hence the symbol *O* was free to be used for another purpose and the Greeks used it to represent the /o/ sound as in our own alphabet.

A similar story can be repeated for the origins of the Greek letter *A* (which came to us unchanged via Latin). The Proto-Sinaitic letter represented a bull's head: ▽. Under the pressure of stylization the eyes disappeared and eventually (through some intervening stages) the letter was turned upside down, ending up as our *A*.

As a result of this process Greek was able to represent vowels alongside the consonants, using the Greek forms *A E H* (= /ē/) *I O* and *Ω* (= /ō/). Thus the Greeks created an alphabet in our modern sense, in which both consonants and vowels are catered for and written on the same line of writing. We will see later that users of other scripts, especially Syriac and Hebrew and Arabic, were aware of the difficulties involved in a consonant-only writing system and made their own attempts to compensate for this by marking vowels above and below the line of writing, but the Greeks solved the problem in a more radical way by inventing letters to represent the vowels alongside the consonants.

The users of the English alphabet are heirs to this combination of Semitic and Greek innovation. The Greek alphabet was transmitted to the Etruscans and Romans and as a result of the extent of the Roman Empire in the West (from the first century CE onwards), the Latin-type alphabet came to be used universally in the West. Some changes were made in the process of dissemination. For example, *W* is a relatively late (eleventh century CE) innovation: it is used in German (for the sound /v/, since *V* in German is used for /f/) and in English, but it does not exist in French and Italian (except in a handful of loan-words). Another innovation, which never happened in any of the Middle Eastern alphabetic scripts, was the creation of distinct lower case and upper case (capital) letters. These are also an important part of our system of punctuation, used to distinguish names from ordinary words and to mark the beginning of a new sentence. Logically the preceding full stop would have been sufficient for this latter purpose and this is how the Middle Eastern scripts eventually came to separate sentences. (The absence of capital letters at the beginning of names can present an obstacle, especially for a slow reader of the Arabic script!)

South Arabia (the Sabaeans, etc.)

There is a much more obscure history behind the transmission of the alphabet to the Sabaean kingdom and the other kingdoms of pre-Islamic Yemen. Although the script used in this region looks superficially very different from scripts like Hebrew and Arabic, there is no doubt that it comes from the same source, the linear alphabet of the late second millennium BCE. The script looks different because it has been stylized to an extreme degree, with vertical and horizontal strokes predominant, especially in the form of the script which is best known, that used in temple and other formal inscriptions (such as the inscriptions on the famous dam at Mārib east of Ṣanʿāʾ). This is the monumental script: in recent times many examples of the cursive script, written on wood, have been found and these do not have the same predominance of vertical and horizontal lines.

Prior to the discovery of these more cursive materials, some scholars believed that the angular form of the south Arabian scripts must have been influenced by awareness of Greek monumental inscriptions: this would lead to chronological consequences, implying a late date for the adoption of the alphabet in south Arabia. There is evidence, however, from Yemen of the alphabet having been adopted soon after 1000 BCE, a conclusion which fits well with the evidence from the Bible and from Assyrian inscriptions that the

Sabaeans were in contact with the Levant long before the rise of the Greeks.

From the southwest corner of Arabia, the alphabetic writing tradition migrated to Ethiopia. Later, in the Christian era, the local Ethiopian script underwent an elaboration whereby the individual consonants could have small flourishes added to them to indicate which vowel was to follow. Thereby an alphabetic syllabary was developed, since each sign ended up standing for a whole syllable. This system is rather complicated. The learner of classical Ethiopic and of modern Amharic (the official language of Ethiopia) has to learn almost 200 signs (though many are very similar to each other, with the variation representing the change of the following vowel).

The Aramaeans

The passing of the alphabet to the Aramaeans was momentous, since subsequent accidents of history resulted in the fact that the three most important Middle Eastern alphabetic scripts owe their origins to the Aramaic version of the alphabet: this applies to the Arabic script, the modern Hebrew script (see above) and the Syriac scripts. Arabic and Hebrew continue in vernacular use, as do their scripts. The Syriac dialects are much more restricted in their use today.

The Aramaeans emerged in the late second millennium BCE, in part filling a power vacuum after the collapse of earlier empires (especially the Hittite Empire) and before the rise of Assyria. They formed kingdoms centred on cities like Damascus and Hamath (Hama), and are frequently mentioned in connection with events in ancient Israel, which was intermittently allied with or subordinated to them. Like Israel, they came later under Assyrian pressure and eventually their independent kingdoms disappeared.

The language used by the Aramaeans is called Aramaic. It is related to the other Semitic languages of the area, though it is quite distinct from them. Like the Israelites, the Aramaeans borrowed the Phoenician alphabet and made it their own. We have extensive royal and official inscriptions in Aramaic from c. 900 BCE onwards. One of the most remarkable was found at Tel Dan in the north of modern Israel: it gives an account of Aramaean victories over the Israelites.

When the Assyrians became fully engaged in empire-building in the western part of the Middle East they made use of Aramaic for diplomatic and practical purposes, employing Aramaean scribes. Aramaeans also spread into Mesopotamia and insinuated themselves into high positions of power. When the Babylonians took over from the Assyrians, for a short time after 612 BCE, Aramaic was even more widespread than before.

The Arrival of the Achaemenid Persians

An unexpected sequence of historical events then turned Aramaic into an international language, a *lingua franca* of the ancient Near East, used extremely widely for diplomacy and commerce and fairly widely also as a spoken vernacular. This series of events began with the overthrow of the Babylonian Empire in 539 BCE by the Persians (the Achaemenid Persians – the title distinguishes their dynasty from several other, later Persian dynasties). Under the new Persian Empire, which extended from the southern limits of Egypt near Elephantine and Aswan to the Bosphorus in the

West and into northern Arabia, the Persian Gulf and north India in the East, Aramaic was used as the language of diplomacy and trade.

As a result of this, Aramaic began to be used even by peoples who spoke other languages in everyday life and the language gained in prestige and importance. Literature began to be written in Aramaic and existing literature was translated into Aramaic (as the Hebrew Bible was a little later). If you had to communicate with the political and legal authorities of the Persian Empire, you had to do so in Aramaic. From Elephantine we have a large archive of Aramaic texts produced by the Judaean colony there, including legal texts and letters of complaint to Persian officials (Illustration 1).

1. Persian Period Aramaic Deed from 402 BCE

From Samaria (the ancient capital of the old Kingdom of Israel) we have legal texts of the Persian period dealing with the buying and selling of slaves. Both of these archives, incidentally, are preserved on papyrus. Papyrus was widely used for writing practical documents, though it does not usually survive well. Aramaic papyri which have survived come mostly from Egypt and Palestine because of favourable climatic conditions.

Aramaic was also used by the Persians for public monuments; inscriptions on stone and significant monuments have been found as far apart as the west coast of Turkey (Xanthos) and the north of what is now Saudi Arabia (Taymā').

This wide usage of Aramaic set the scene for its script to be transformed into some of the best-known alphabetic scripts of the Middle East. In the Persian era, the international Aramaic used for official purposes and the script in which it was written were fairly homogeneous, but when Alexander the Great destroyed the Persian Empire in 330 BCE, he (or rather his successor kings, the Seleucids and Ptolemies) replaced Aramaic with Greek as an official language. Thus the homogeneous Aramaic of the Persians did not need to be homogeneous any more and it split into a large number of dialects with corresponding variations of script.

The circumstances were different in different areas.

In Jerusalem and Palestine, Hebrew gave way to Aramaic as the predominant language in the last centuries BCE. Parts of the Book of Daniel and the Book of Ezra are actually *written* in Aramaic, while the decline of knowledge of Hebrew was such that it became the habit to provide a running translation into Aramaic when the Bible was being read in public.

Eventually (as already noted) the Aramaic script, which had become virtually universal, replaced the old script used for copies of the Hebrew Bible (though the language remained Hebrew) and this Jewish Aramaic script, with its own peculiarities, came to be regarded as the "Hebrew" script. Literature began to be composed in Aramaic by Jews, as we see in texts among the Dead Sea Scrolls. Legal transactions were conducted in Aramaic, as the Jewish papyri from the Dead Sea area show. Even marriage documents were drawn up in Aramaic (and still are).

Further north, in the Syrian desert, the ancient trading city of Palmyra began to use its own dialect of Aramaic and Aramaic script just before the Roman Period and several thousand inscriptions have survived. Being under heavy Roman influence the Palmyrenes also used Greek and many of the inscriptions are bilingual. Palmyra was effectively destroyed in 272 CE and its script and dialect disappeared.

To its northeast, the desert city of Hatra adopted a local dialect of Aramaic and a distinctive version of the script as an official language, while further south, in Mesopotamia, the Jewish community (numerically very substantial) used a Mesopotamian dialect of Aramaic, composing theological works and generating the Babylonian Talmud. Also in southern Mesopotamia from around the time of Christ were the Mandaeans, a religious group who used Aramaic and devised their own modified version of the script. They still survive (often called Sabians) though in much depleted numbers.

Apart from the Jewish script and the Mandaean, only two other scripts which emerged in the post-Persian period continued and generated an important later history, the Syriac and the Nabataean.

Syriac

One of the urban centres left to its own devices by the Seleucid regime in Syria was the city and kingdom of Edessa, modern Urfa or Şanliurfa in southern Turkey. A local dynasty ruled it from about 132 BCE and since it was traditionally an Aramaic-speaking region, the local dynasty adopted the local dialect rather than Greek as its official language. Inscriptions began to be made in this language, which came eventually to be known as Syriac (though the title Edessan Aramaic is perfectly satisfactory for the earlier period). Most of the inscriptions are dated to the first two centuries CE and to the early years of the Roman occupation of Edessa in the third century CE.

However, Syriac was destined to take on a life of its own, independently of these modest beginnings, since Edessa was converted to Christianity and Syriac became a church language. The date of the conversion is put by legend in the first century CE, but a more likely time for the official adoption of Christianity as the state religion is the early third century CE. By the latter date the Old Testament had been largely translated into Syriac (perhaps originally by local Jews) and then the Greek New Testament. This Syriac New Testament was the first Semitic-language translation of the Christian scriptures and apart from satisfying the needs of the local Christians, it also became popular among the many other Aramaic-speaking Christians of the Fertile Crescent, from the Persian Gulf to Palestine. This had the effect of spreading the Edessan dialect and its local script over a wide area: the spread is somewhat analogous to the spread of Arabic with the Quran to areas which had not been previously Arabic-speaking.

Other works were also translated from Greek into Syriac and the Syriac-speaking churches (later divided on sectarian grounds into western and eastern branches) embarked on a thousand-year scholarly, mostly theological, enterprise which only petered out eventually in the thirteenth century (and even then not completely). The literature produced in Syriac during this time was vast: hundreds of books by major theologians and historians, many of them still unpublished, though surviving in manuscript form. The British Library, for example, has a magnificent collection.

The Syriac church community was affected by the theological controversies in the Christian church in the fourth and fifth centuries. This resulted in a partial separation of western Christians in Syria and eastern Christians in Iraq. The two dialects were only marginally different, with eastern /ā/ pronounced as /o/ in the West, but the styles of writing the Syriac script eventually differed considerably. There were three main script-forms: the *estrangela* script (traditional, similar to the script of the early inscriptions, used by both communities), the eastern script (used solely by the eastern branch of the church) and the *serta* (with its origins in the early cursive script used on soft materials, e.g. for legal purposes [Illustration 2], and confined later to the western Syriac church).

This Syriac script in its three forms was derived from the Aramaic script of the Achaemenid period (which in turn

2. Syriac Legal Parchment of 243 CE

was derived from the older Aramaic script of the Assyrian period).

Like the other scripts of this alphabetic tradition, the Syriac script was basically consonantal, though the disadvantage of not being able to represent vowels properly had prompted the users of several of the scripts (Aramaic initially, but later Hebrew) to develop ways of clarifying what vowel should be read in certain circumstances. The technique used was that of allowing three of the existing consonantal signs to stand not only for a consonant, but also for an associated vowel. Thus the Aramaic y came to be used to represent a long /ī/ and sometimes long /ē/; ' to represent long /ā/ and sometimes long /ē/; and w to represent long /ū/ and sometimes long /ō/. In other words y could stand either for the consonant /y/ or the vowel /ī/. This is a bit like the difference between the y in English "yet" (where it stands for a consonant) and the y in English "truly" (where it stands for a vowel). This system of marking vowels was ambiguous and incomplete (no short vowels were covered by it), but it became deeply entrenched in the writing systems used for both Aramaic (including Syriac) and Hebrew. In both Hebrew and Syriac the traditional text of the Bible was written using these extra values for the letters in question. It thus became a fixed part of the orthography of both languages. Orthography means "standardized, correct way of writing", effectively "traditional spelling". It is orthography which determines the fact in English that so many words are spelled in peculiar ways: "cough" (instead of "coff"), "through" (instead of "thru"), "sugar" (instead of "shugar"). These English orthographic conventions normally arise from the history of the words in question and represent what is called "historical spelling".

The point to note here, however, is that such spelling conventions are extremely conservative and almost impossible to reform (except perhaps under a totalitarian regime). Imagine the political fuss which would be caused in Britain or France if it were suggested that there should be a spelling reform to make everything easier for children and foreigners!

There is an important point here in relation to the next big stage in the development of the Syriac and Hebrew scripts. In church circles and in rabbinic circles there was a full awareness of the inadequacies of the existing ways of marking vowels. Religious leaders in particular were concerned that the Scriptures, the word of God, were in danger of being mispronounced, misread, misunderstood and misinterpreted. There was a right way and a wrong way to pronounce the vowels of the text, but there was no systematic way of indicating the right pronunciation to the reader who would recite the text in the synagogue or church.

Distinguishing between Consonants

Both the Jewish Aramaic and the Syriac scripts had had minor problems with letters which were indistinguishable. In Jewish Aramaic (and Hebrew), the letter שׁ had for historical reasons come to stand both for /š/ (= /sh/) and for /ś/ (= /s/, though originally pronounced distinctly). This created an ambiguity in the script which was resolved by the introduction of diacritic dots: שׁ = š; שׂ = ś. A similar situation pertained in Syriac with regard to d and r. The two letters had ended up looking identical and were then distinguished by the addition of dots: ܕ = d; ܪ = r.

Vocalization and other Diacritics

Both Jews and Christians devised new systems to solve the major problems still remaining. It appears that Christians started the idea, but that is not 100 per cent certain, and in any case the idea was soon taken up by Jews too. The basic solution was the same in each case, the addition of signs above and below the consonants to indicate which vowel was to be pronounced after it. Why, you may ask, did they not do what the Greeks did and invent vowel signs which would sit on the same line as the consonants? The answer seems to be the same in both the Jewish and the Christian case: the sacred text of the Bible was already established and fixed, with fixed orthography – it would be unthinkable to start rewriting the word of God according to a new writing convention. So instead the marks were added above and below the line of writing.

The discussion here will not go into the detail of the system devised for Hebrew: it has no direct bearing on the rest of this book. Suffice it to note that the Hebrew system (or systems, since there were initially several) is highly complex. For example, a special sign was devised to indicate the *absence* of a vowel after a consonant, a feature which is found later in Arabic vocalization. The complexity of the Hebrew "pointing" (as it is called) is such that its study is a distinct field of specialization within Hebrew and Jewish Studies and even a teacher of Biblical Hebrew who has been teaching the language and reading texts with students for years is unlikely to have a detailed knowledge of the marks. In practice this does not create a major problem, since the full complex system was only ever applied to the Bible, not to the writing of Hebrew for ordinary purposes.

We now turn to the case of the Syriac vocalization systems.

Early attempts to resolve ambiguities in Syriac texts took the form of adding dots above and below the line to distinguish words which are otherwise spelled identically in consonantal script. Thus the sequence of letters *qtl* could be pronounced *qtal* or *qātel* and they have different meanings ("he killed" and "killing"). A dot came to be placed over the *qtl* when it was to be pronounced *qātel* and this is a common ambiguity with different verbal roots, so it solved one problem. Ambiguous singulars and plurals were disambiguated by placing a double dot sign over plurals: the dots were not vowel indicators, but gave the reader the information needed for correct reading. Thus *mlk'* could be singular *malkā* or plural *malkē*: the double-dot sign would make it clear that *malkē* was intended. Certain consonants which could be pronounced in two variant ways depending on circumstances were distinguished again by the use of a dot above or below (so, for example, *p* would be pronounced /f/ if there was a vowel before it).

Eventually all this was systematized and in addition a series of vowel markers was devised. In the West Syriac tradition miniature forms of the Greek vowels *A O E H* and *OU* (combined) were used to represent the main vowels /a/ /o/ /e/ /ī/ /ū/ and each could be placed either above or below the consonant after which the vowel was to be pronounced. This did not interfere with the existing sequence of consonants and it allowed the older system of the double use of *y ' w* to remain undisturbed.

While adequate, this system was far from perfect: the East Syrian system is marginally better. It consists of dots (not of miniature Greek letters) placed in fixed positions to indicate the vowels: e.g. a double dot above indicates /ā/, while a single dot above accompanied by a single dot below indicates /a/.

Syriac manuscripts frequently have the vowel marks in a different colour from the main consonantal text, and they have often been added by a different hand at a different time from the original.

This completes our survey of the earlier alphabetic writing systems and their vocalization strategies in the pre-Islamic and pre-Arabic phase of our history. There is only one important omission, that of the Nabataean writing system. Since the Nabataean script probably lies at the origin of the Arabic script, it is dealt with in the next chapter alongside the emergence of the Arabic script itself.

II - The Origin of the Arabic Alphabet

Where did the Arabic alphabet come from? It is the intention of this chapter to answer this question, explaining the link between earlier alphabets described in the last chapter and the elaboration of the basic Arabic alphabet which will be pursued in chapters III and following.

As so often in historical discussions of this kind, there is not a complete consensus on the interpretation of the evidence and as a result two different answers have been promulgated in recent times. Both see the Arabic alphabet emerging from writing systems already in existence in the Middle East in continuity with what we have seen in Chapter I.

The predominant view is that the Arabic alphabet is best explained as a development from the Nabataean alphabet of the first few centuries CE. This view is adopted here and will form the basis of this chapter. The other view is that the Syriac alphabet had a central role in the creation of the Arabic alphabet. This hypothesis will be briefly outlined at the end of the chapter.

The Nabataeans and their Alphabet

The Nabataean kingdom was centred on Petra in modern Jordan. It existed as an independent state from at least the fourth century BCE and at times extended to include southern Syria, the Negev of southern Palestine, parts of Sinai and the northern Hijaz. The kingdom came to an end in 106 CE, when the last Nabataean king died and the kingdom was incorporated by the Romans into the "Province of Arabia". The Nabataeans did not immediately disappear and Petra continued to be an important city within the Roman and later Byzantine administrations.

The inhabitants of Nabataea were very varied. Many of them, especially those in the northern areas of the kingdom, were Aramaic-speakers. Others, in northern Arabia and eastern Jordan, spoke languages closely related to Arabic (though, of course, there is no direct and clear evidence of Arabic itself, in the form of inscriptions in Arabic script, until some time after the end of the Nabataean kingdom). For example, the so-called Safaitic inscriptions of eastern Jordan are written in a language akin to, though not identical with, the later Arabic. While there is considerable uncertainty about which group of Nabataean citizens spoke which language, what is completely clear is that for *inscriptions* and for *legal transactions* the Nabataeans used Aramaic, albeit a rather archaic dialect of Aramaic. Aramaic had this public role because, as we have seen, it had become a *lingua franca* throughout the Fertile Crescent: in other words it was a well-established prestige language which was turned to for official purposes, a bit like Latin in early Medieval Europe, before languages like English were used in formal contexts.

The number of surviving Nabataean inscriptions is very large, around 6,000, though many are very short and contain little more than personal names. Fortunately there is a smaller number of longer and more complicated inscriptions, many of them from tombs and temples, and in addition there have been published in recent years a number of Nabataean legal papyri, some of which are very long indeed (Illustrations 3, 4, 5).

When copies of the inscriptions were first brought to Europe in the late eighteenth century, scholars had difficulty deciphering them. The reason for the difficulty turned out

3. Nabataean Monumental Inscription from Madā'in Ṣāliḥ, Saudi Arabia, dated 49/50 CE

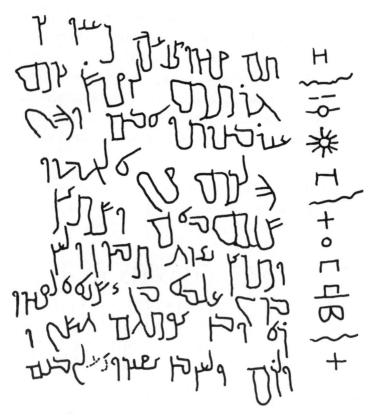

4. The Nabataean-Arabic Raqūsh Inscriptions from Madā'in Ṣāliḥ, Saudi Arabia, dated 268 CE

to be the fact that the Nabataean alphabetic script had diverged considerably from its parent script of the Achaemenid Persian period (see Chapter I). This meant that the script of the Nabataean inscriptions did not look much like the Aramaic or Hebrew or Syriac scripts. Eventually in 1840 it was deciphered by Eduard Beer of Leipzig and it was then clear that it was another local variant of the older Aramaic script,

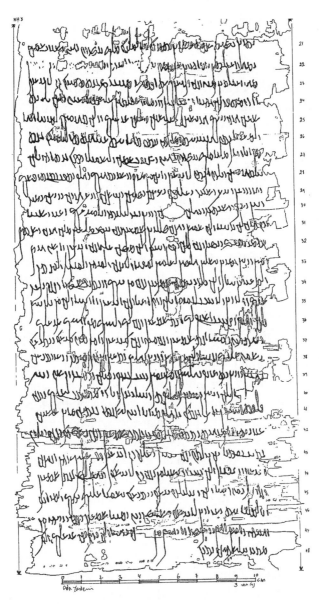

5. Nabataean Legal Papyrus, dated 97/98 CE

like the Jewish script (now used for Hebrew), Syriac, Palmyrene, etc.

Linguistically it also became clear that there was some Arabic-type influence in the Nabataean inscriptions, items of vocabulary which were unknown in the Aramaic dialects, but found in later Arabic sources. This Arabic influence in the Aramaic of Nabataea confirms the general impression that the Nabataean elite had close connections with northern Arabia, as seen from personal names (such as Sa'adallāhī) and religion (worship of Dushara, Allāt, al-'Uzzā). In the early study of the Nabataean inscriptions, however, there was little attention paid to the similarities between the Nabataean and Arabic scripts. The main reason for this was the fact that the main inscriptions found at Petra and other sites (such as Madā'in Ṣāliḥ in Saudi Arabia) were written in a monumental form of the Nabataean script. Awareness of the fact that there were various forms of the Nabataean script is relatively recent.

The monumental script (Illustration 3), which is sometimes made elegant (calligraphic) by the elongatation and making parallel of vertical lines, appears to hang by the top of each letter from a horizontal line, an aspect which is unusual in the various forms of the late Aramaic script. Letters are not in principle joined to each other, though they sometimes touch each other more or less accidentally. With one or two exceptions the forms of the letters are standardized by the first century CE (the period of most of the inscriptions). The one letter which varies considerably is the first letter of the alphabet, transliterated as ' and called in Arabic *alif*. (The Arabic names of the letters are used for convenience, since the assumption will be made that most readers of this will be interested primarily in the Arabic script which eventually emerged.) For this letter there are two very different-looking forms, ⌒ and ◊ . The former of these is not unlike the Hebrew א. The other form is a stylized version of the same basic letter: it is turned into an oval shape with an upper stroke. It was this monumental script which was deciphered in 1840 by Beer.

A second form of script is found in the thousands of Nabataean graffiti on rock-faces. What seems to be happening here is that a more cursive form of writing, such as might be used on papyrus or other soft materials (such as parchment, made from animal skin), is intruding into an attempt by the writer to produce a monumental inscription style. The modern analogy here is the commonly seen handwritten notice, e.g. in a shop window, which often produces a clumsy imitation of a properly printed notice. The graffiti, especially common in Sinai, rarely contain much more than the name of the writer and his father, alongside an imprecation asking for blessing. A few are more complicated and contain historical allusions. But so far as the history of the script is concerned, these meagre data provide a mine of information.

The fact that there were also cursive Nabataean scripts with systematic joining of letters and a high degree of stylization did not become clear until a Nabataean papyrus text was published in 1954. This and most of the Nabataean papyri discovered subsequently were legal texts and one can easily imagine their being produced by a local scribe in a small town, using a well-established cursive script, written quickly with the pen hardly being taken off the page (Illustration 5). Naturally these cursive forms of Nabataean writing are much more difficult for us to read: analysis involves a painstaking word by word division of the text, as well as the problems arising from damaged portions of text.

Despite the fact that some letters in the cursive script are very hard to distinguish from each other, there is only very late evidence (third century) of any use of diacritics to distinguish letters. As in the case of Syriac, *d* and *r* cause particular problems and there are a few late Nabataean inscriptions which place a dot over the *d* to identify it. (Recall that in Syriac a dot is placed *below* the letter to identify it.) It seems that the *concept* of introducing diacritics existed long before they were used to systematize the Arabic script, though there is no connection between the way they are used for Arabic and the ways they were used for Nabataean and Syriac.

It is from the close consideration of the individual letters of cursive Nabataean, rather than the monumental script (though consideration of the monumental script does contribute), that we are led to the conclusion that there must be a historical connection between the Nabataean and Arabic scripts. We will be using the cursive Arabic of the early papyri from the seventh century (see Chapter IV) as the basis of comparison with the Nabataean, though for practical reasons the ordinary (*naskhī*) printed forms are cited in the discussion. (For Arabic papyrus forms see Illustration 6.) At the end of this chapter we will take the story forward to trace the evidence for the continued use of the Nabataean script long after the disappearance of the Nabataean kingdom. The next chapter will take up the earliest use of the Nabataean-type script for writing Arabic.

The reader can make his or her own study by comparing the letter-forms in the accompanying chart (Illustration 6). Here we select the more obvious similarities.

Transliter-ation	Printed Jewish Aramaic	Early Syriac Cursive	Printed estrangela Syriac	Monumental Nabataean	Cursive Nabataean	Early Arabic Papyri	Printed Arabic (most relevant form is cited)
ʾ	א						ا
b	ב						ب
g	ג						ج
d	ד						د
h	ה						ه
w	ו						و
z	ז						ز
ḥ	ח						ح
ṭ	ט						ط
y	י						ي
k	כ						ك
l	ל						ل
m	מ						م
n	נ						ن
s	ס						
ʿ	ע						ع
p	פ						ف
ṣ	צ						ص
q	ק						ق
r	ר						ر
š	ש/שׂ						س
t	ת						ت

6. Nabataean, Aramaic and Syriac Scripts

A good example to start with is the letter ʿ*ayin* which has been mentioned earlier. It had its origin as a circle with a dot in the middle (Proto-Sinaitic); then the dot disappeared (Phoenician etc.) and the circle was written in two strokes leading to 𐤏 . In the Aramaic script, a gap began to appear at the top and this led to the Aramaic and Hebrew form 𝕐 (with a continuation line to the left). The well-known Arabic form of this letter is ع (here printed in the form it has when it is joined to a following letter: its free-standing and "final" forms are ع ع) showing a certain resemblance to 𝕐, but the missing link between the two is provided by the Nabataean form 𝒴 (which appears universally in the Nabataean cursive and frequently in the Nabataean monumental). Both the Nabataean and the Arabic forms are distinctive in turning the basic shape of the letter into a kind of curved hook with a continuation stroke leading down to the line of writing. A glance at the comparative chart which also shows the Syriac form of the same letter (ܥ) reveals that it is *only* in Nabataean and Arabic that this hooking takes place. Finally, of course, Arabic used this letter to represent two different consonants (ʿ*ayn* and *ghayn*), only one of which existed in Aramaic (ʿ*ayn*). In order to do this effectively a diacritic was needed (ع غ).

Similar arguments apply to the development of the following letter-forms. (The details on these next few pages may be skipped by readers who are already convinced by the example of ʿ*ayin*.)

א / ا

The letter called in Arabic *alif* has a complex X-form in earlier scripts (a form which goes back to the bull-pictograph described earlier). In monumental Nabataean it often has this form, especially at the ends of words. Another form, which seems to be a stylized version of this, developed: ◖. Both of these forms look widely different from the later Arabic *alif* (ı). When we look, however, at the Nabataean cursive we find that both in the papyri and in the graffiti the letter is often reduced in form to a vertical line. (Syriac *estrangela* script retains features of the older shape of the letter: ✓, though there is a vertical line final form in early Syriac cursive.)

ב / ب

Arabic *bā'*, as with many Arabic letters, looks rather different in its non-joined-up and joined-up forms: ب ـب (the diacritic dot can be ignored for the moment: it was introduced later, when several letter-forms became ambiguous). In the older Aramaic script the letter consisted of three sides of a square, with an opening on the left side: ⏋. This form is retained in monumental Nabataean, but in the cursive form the letter rotates in a clockwise direction so that the opening is at the top. The shape becomes more rounded where the letter appears unconnected to what follows (ٮ), while being reduced to a single "peak" on the line of writing if there is something following (ـٮ). (Syriac retains the older form, though elongated: ⎓ .)

ג / ج

The letter *jīm* is non-diagnostic, meaning that the evidence does not tell us much beyond the fact that the Nabataean letter (⟍) can be seen to be a possible ancestor of the Arabic (ج ح). (Syriac ⟍ .)

ד / د

It is a similar situation for *dāl* and *dhāl*: cursive Nabataean ﴿ comparable with Arabic (joined-up) form ﺪ .

ה / ة

In the case of the Arabic letter *hā'* one can point to the final form of the letter which appears in cursive Nabataean: ∝. This is an unexpected transformation of the basic form of the Nabataean letter as ⵍ (final ∬), but it shows a high degree of continuity with Arabic *hā'*, especially in its final form: ﺔ . (*Esṭrangela* Syriac ന; Western Syriac and early cursive ന .)

ו / و

In the case of *wāw* the early Aramaic form of the letter was rather like the Greek capital *u*: Υ. In due course the upper right-hand stroke was lost and in monumental Nabataean the letter is a vertical with a hook to the left at the top. In the cursive script this hook was closed to form a loop and the whole letter became more rounded, ending up almost identical with Arabic ﻮ . (In Syriac the letter became a simple circle: ၈ .)

ז / ر

Zāy is non-diagnostic so far as the transition from Nabataean to Arabic is concerned. It has the form of a short vertical line, later curved as ﺝ. This form is compatible with the Arabic form (ﺰ).

П / ح

Arabic *ḥā'* and *khā'* came to have their form (later distinguished through use of the diacritic) through a sequence of change starting with monumental Nabataean: Л > Л . (The Syriac form is quite different, basically ﯨ in all three scripts.)

ٻ / ط

Ṭā' (from which *ẓā'* was derived) in monumental Nabataean is not unlike the "Hebrew" letter ⟆, but this developed in the cursive into a form with a closed loop on the right and a near vertical stroke on the left: ⟆ . This in turn approximates to the Arabic ط. (The Syriac letter is very different, extending below the line of writing: ⟋ .)

◗ / ي

Monumental Nabataean *yā'* is similar to the Jewish Aramaic form: ⟋, written "in mid air" above the line. This is a little different from the Arabic letter, which sits on the line, though the Arabic final form, ي ى , has antecedents in the final-form cursive Nabataean ⟅ . (Syriac ﯨ sits on the line.)

⊃ / ك

Kāf had developed ultimately from a Phoenician letter which looks like a reversed *K*, and this betrays the origin of our letter *K*. In Aramaic it came to have a form similar to *bā'*, though with rounded corners, as in the Hebrew form. In Nabataean the upper line tended to turn upwards quite sharply: ⌐ and there was a final form in which the lower line became vertical: ⌐ . The Arabic form, ك, appears to be based on this pattern (while the Syriac retains the older form: ܐ).

ל / ل

The "bulge" to the right of the *lām*, an earlier characteristic of this letter, often preserved in Nabataean (and even exaggerated, perhaps for artistic effect), is in fact commonly straightened in graffiti and papyri so that it becomes a simple vertical line, as in Arabic: ل . (In Syriac it is slopes at almost 45 degrees: ܠ .)

מ / م

In some examples the monumental Nabataean *mīm* is almost identical to the Jewish Aramaic form, but it varies considerably and in more cursive writing it frequently opens up at the upper left corner so that it can be written in a single movement of the pen (ܒ) or is turned into a small angular circle sitting on the line of writing (ܩ). In this form it is very similar to the Arabic form ܡ (final م).

נ / ن

The letter, called in Arabic *nūn*, consisted originally of a vertical line with a leftward extension at the top. In the Jewish Aramaic script, an extension along the line of writing was added at the bottom, while in Nabataean monumental script there was a leftward extension at the bottom only: ܠ. In the cursive script the letter was reduced to a short vertical, very difficult to distinguish from *bā'* except when final. Final *nūn* appears as a vertical extending well below the line of writing: ܉.

ס

This letter has no equivalent in Arabic: Arabic used its own version of שׁ (below) to represent a simple /s/, i.e. it used the letter called *sīn*.

ע / ع

See page 60.

פ / ف

The traditional *fāʾ* (actually normally pronounced *p* as in "pit", though in certain circumstances it could be pronounced as *f* as in "often") had its upper loop open (as in Hebrew). Monumental Nabataean retains this feature, but in cursive script it tends to be closed and sometimes the whole letter is rounded: ܩ. It thus resembles the Arabic form apart from the diacritic (ف). (Syriac also has it closed: ܦ.)

צ / ص

The traditional Aramaic forms behind Arabic *ṣād* (and, of course, *ḍād*) and *qāf* are very similar: ܖ. They were distinguishable in Nabataean through the fact that in *qāf* the loop was closed, while in *ṣād* it was usually left open and the top of the letter was angular and had a small projection at the top to the left: ܟ . In the earliest Arabic forms we find a closed loop with the projection on the left, later ص. (The Syriac is completely different: ܨ .)

ק / ق

Continuing from what is stated above, the closed circle at the top of the letter became standard in Nabataean and this became the characteristic shape of *qāf*, as reflected also in Syriac (‌). Here the Nabataean characteristic of the loop being raised above the line, with an attached descending stroke, is preserved in Arabic ق : the letter now sits on the line and had to be distinguished from *fā'* by the use of diacritics.

٦ / ر

As has been noted earlier, in older Aramaic scripts, including Nabataean, there was a tendency for *rā'* and *dāl* to end up looking identical. This can be seen from the printed Hebrew forms given. As we have seen, they were distinguished in Syriac (and extremely rarely in Nabataean) by the use of a diacritic. In Arabic this letter had a different trajectory. Having turned clockwise onto its back, it ended up identical with *zāy* and had to be distinguished from it by use of a diacritic.

שׁ שׂ שׁ / ش س

The traditional Aramaic *šīn* (*shīn*)/*śīn* had two pronunciations (arising from a complex detail of linguistic history which need not detain us here). In the form of the script used by Jews the two were distinguished by a diacritic placed on the right (for *š*) and on the left (for *ś*, which was in the period we are discussing pronounced simply as /s/). So effectively the letter could stand for *š* or *s*. The Arabic reflects exactly the same situation, with diacritics distinguishing the two: س ش . (The Syriac form is different, though it has the same origin and one can see a certain similarity: ‌ .)

ת / ت

Arabic *tā'* and *thā'* do not look at all like the Aramaic form represented here by the Hebrew printed letter. The Syriac looks slightly more like the Aramaic (ܐ). The discrepancy is, however, deceptive. While the Nabataean monumental form is rather similar to the older Aramaic (ת), in cursive writing it often falls over to the right and the left-hand vertical (vertical in the Aramaic) gets shortened, so that we end up with ﻭ . From this it is but a short step to the basic shape of the letter found in Arabic: ﺣ . Diacritics were needed to separate *t* from *th* (ﺛ) (and also the *bā'*: ﺑ).

It thus appears that so far as the majority of the Arabic letters is concerned (though stripped of the diacritic dots, which were not needed for Nabataean, since Nabataean had the sounds of Aramaic, not the sounds of Arabic), there is a very close resemblance with the cursive form of Nabataean used in papyrus documents.

At this point we need to point forward to the earliest documentary Arabic texts, papyri from Egypt in the seventh century CE.

Of course there is a gap of several hundred years between the Nabataean kingdom and the early Islamic period. However, the Nabataean script continued in active use for a long time after the fall of the kingdom. We know this from dated texts in the second and third centuries CE. There are, for example, dated inscriptions like the so-called Raqūsh inscription at Madā'in Ṣāliḥ, dated 268 CE (Illustration 4), and two or three others from around 300 CE. The latest dated Nabataean inscription is from the same area and dates to 356 CE.

While this reduces the gap between the latest Nabataean and the earliest Arabic papyri, it does not remove it completely, leaving about 300 years to be accounted for. We must assume that during this 300-year period the Nabataean script was continuing in use on papyrus. There was no Nabataean state, but the script would have been used for practical purposes by merchants.

Occasionally we get glimpses of the Nabataean script being used to write the Arabic language. There is part of a first-century CE inscription from Nabataean 'Avdat in Israel which appears to be in Arabic, despite the script being Nabataean. Clearer is the inscription dated 268 CE referred to above (Illustration 4). And finally, completely clear is the Arabic tomb inscription of Imru' al-Qays from Namāra in southern Syria (328 CE). This is in presentable classical Arabic, though the script is again Nabataean.

Of a slightly later date are several other inscriptions which are usually counted among the first Arabic inscriptions (see chapter III). They are mostly short and in a rather angular script which owes something to the Nabataean, but may also be influenced by Syriac: most come from Syria where Syriac had become a major ecclesiastical language in the late pre-Islamic period.

The Question of the Role of the Syriac Script

There is no doubt that the Muslim Arabs, as they expanded into Syria, will have encountered the Syriac script. Already this script had a long tradition behind it. One of the finest Syriac calligraphic manuscripts is dated 411 CE (Illustration 7). It seems probable, therefore, that the Syriac script will have

7. Syriac Manuscript, dated 411 CE

had some impact. For example, the use of a diacritic mark to distinguish Syriac *d* and *r* (**ܖ** and **ܕ**) was already well established and this may have given rise to the idea of adding dots to various inherited Aramaic letters in order to distinguish letters which had ended up looking the same, such as ب and ت and ث, and to mark distinctively consonants which exist in Arabic but did not exist in the earlier languages which used the script (e.g. *ghayn* and *khā'*, to distinguish them from *'ayn* and *ḥā'*: غ خ). We have already seen that Syriac was in the process of developing a system of vowel signs and other marks to distinguish words from one another.

It is not unreasonable, therefore, to entertain the possibility that the Arabic script might have been devised on the basis of copying Syriac. This view was espoused by one of the greatest modern Nabataean scholars, Jean Starcky. The one telling argument in favour of this viewpoint has been the observation that the Arabic script and the Syriac script share the feature of "sitting" on the line of writing: that is, the engraver of an inscription and the scribe of a manuscript either draws or imagines a horizontal line and the letters sit on top of that line (Illustrations 2 and 7). In Nabataean the situation is more complex. Often, in inscriptions on stone, it appears that the Nabataean script is suspended from the horizontal line and indeed there are occasionally traces of lines on the stone, created to help the carver (e.g. inscription H 30 at Madā'in Ṣāliḥ). The result in some inscriptions is that the Nabataean letters look like washing: items of different lengths hanging from a fixed line.

However, this is not a decisive argument. While it is true that in inscriptions on stone there is a tendency to hang the letters from a line, this is not so in the most cursive forms of writing (Illustration 5). There the letters sit on a line in exactly the same way as Syriac and Arabic. Our argument above has been that the Arabic script appearing in early papyri was based on that of Nabataean-script commercial and practical documents, not from copying Nabataean monumental inscriptions.

If we return finally to the shapes of the letters, which are more decisive in this discussion, we can draw up an inventory of those Arabic letters which are close *only* to Nabataean precursors and those which are close to Syriac *and* Nabataean, with the following result:

Arabic similar to Nabataean *only*	Arabic similar to Syriac *and* Nabataean
	ʾ
b	
	g
	d
ḥ	
	w
	z
	ḥ
ṭ	
y	
	k
l	
m	
	n
ʿ	
	p
ṣ	
	q
	r
š	
t	

On this basis a very strong case can be made for the origin of the Arabic script in the Nabataean cursive.

This does not mean that the Syriac script has had no impact. Several forms of the Arabic script developed and it is quite possible that some of them were influenced by Syriac. The Kufic script, for example, is quite different from the *naskhī* script. Its firm rootedness to the line of writing and its angular forms could have been inspired by *estrangela* Syriac. As already noted, the idea of diacritics may have been taken over from Syriac – they barely appear at all in Nabataean. The calligraphic tradition of Syriac may have prompted the beginnings of Arabic calligraphy, an Islamic art in which the Muslims could outperform the Christians.

Dates of Major Developments

1700-1500 BCE	Beginning of alphabetic writing, Palestine, Sinai, Lebanese coast
1200 BCE -	Adoption of linear alphabet by Phoenicians
1000 BCE -	Dissemination of alphabetic writing to Israelites, Moabites, Aramaeans, etc.
700 BCE -	Aramaic script used by Assyrians
539 BCE -	Aramaic as *lingua franca* under Persians
330 BCE -	Local Aramaic scripts develop in Syria, Palestine, etc.
100 BCE -	Nabataean script evidence: monumental and cursive
106 CE +	Continued use of Nabataean script
250-350 CE	Nabataean script being used to write Arabic
300 CE +	Inscriptions in Arabic script begin to appear
643 CE +	First surviving texts on papyrus in Arabic
700 CE +	Surviving Quran fragments
Thereafter	Arabic script becomes commonplace

III - The Earliest Arabic Scripts – Pre- and Early Islamic Inscriptions

In the first two chapters we have considered the basic principles behind the alphabet and the history of alphabetic scripts in the pre-Islamic period. Chapter II has suggested that the best explanation of the origins of the early script of the Arabic papyri is to be found in the cursive Nabataean script. In continuing this discussion, we now consider some of the earliest evidence of the writing of Arabic itself.

As we have seen, our quest to locate and to trace the development of the early Arabic script begins in pre-Islamic times, in the third century CE to be precise, with a series of lapidary inscriptions found in the area of Greater Syria and the northern Arabian Peninsula. The term "lapidary" refers to writings on stone (Latin *lapidarius*, "related to stone"), often brief and formalized.

From time immemorial, humans had been committing their thoughts to the stone all around them which nature had provided in massive quantities. In the various dialects of Aramaic (see Chapter II) and in the languages of pre-Islamic Arabia, Safaitic, Lihyanite, Thamudic etc., desert travellers, local passers-by and herders had been recording their journeys, remembering their dead, or perhaps recording the building of a permanent structure. These are the texts by means of which we can seek to illustrate how the Arabic script which is familiar to us today slowly developed from its immediate Nabataean predecessor.

Twenty or so such lapidary inscriptions which have a bearing on the origin of the Arabic script are now available to us in scholarly studies, some only one or two words long, others of greater length. These inscriptions, the earliest of which are in the Nabataean language, show clear signs that the script is developing into the Arabic script that we recognize today, although dots to distinguish otherwise identical letters are not yet to be found. The most famous inscription of this group by far is the so-called Namāra inscription which can be dated precisely to 328 CE and a very great deal of ink has been spilt over the years in trying to provide some definitive reading. However, of major interest there is mention in the text of the famous king of Kinda, Imru' al-Qays, and, if we could be surer of the meaning, its historical potential must surely be immense.

However, there is no doubt that the 268 CE Raqūsh funerary inscription, a funerary document at Madā'in Ṣāliḥ in present-day Saudi Arabia (Illustration 4), is written primarily in Arabic with a few Aramaisms (like the date for example) and that it is the earliest dated Arabic document so far uncovered. The script, however, remains Nabataean and we cannot yet begin to recognize distinct Arabic script-forms.

At about the same time as the Namāra inscription was being produced, the first inscription which shows clear resemblance to the Arabic script came into being (Illustration 8). It was

8. Jabal Ramm, 300-350 CE

found in Jabal Ramm near Aqaba and can be safely dated to the first half of the fourth century CE. A precise description of the script is difficult, for the text is written with some square features typical of epigraphic Arabic, and yet the fourth line appears more cursive. In particular, one can discern an Arabic final *hā'*, medial *lām*, followed by *yā'* and final *mīm*. An initial *jīm/hā'/khā'*, an initial *alif-lām* and a word which appears to begin with *mīm, sīn/shīn, alif* can be seen.

A tentative leap into the fifth, perhaps the sixth, century is now necessary and we arrive at the important stepping stone of Umm al-Jimāl (Illustration 9) with its distinctly square features. The stone slab on which the inscription appears has been damaged and covered with plaster, but here one can clearly read the name *'Abd Allah bn* (i.e. *ibn*) *'Ubayd*. An *alif-lām* and what could be the Arabic word *'alā*, as well as final *mīm*, can be read.

To complete the survey of pre-Islamic Arabic inscriptions, that of Harran should mentioned, with the clear date 568 CE.

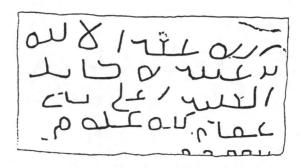

9. Umm al-Jimāl, fifth or sixth Century CE

It is a Greek-Arabic bilingual inscription on the martyrion of St John, containing the name Sharāḥīl bar Ẓālim.

Our story now moves on into the Islamic era. In 2002, what is so far the earliest Islamic Arabic inscription was discovered in the south-west of Saudi Arabia. It is dated 23/643-4 (i.e. AH 23 = 643-4 CE). It is a simple four-word graffito with a clear date. The script is a square Kufic with no dots to distinguish letters. The University of Riyad Department of Archaeology has long been excavating along the Iraqi pilgrim route in Saudi Arabia and in 1977 there was published as part of their data a dated Arabic inscription of 56/676. With little effort, the following features can be made out: initial *alif,* with its hook at the bottom of the letter turning to the right, initial and medial *lām,* medial *ḥā'* and final *mīm* (without a tail), here and in the third word; initial *ghayn,* medial *fā'* and final *rā'* which is to be compared with the final *dāl* in the following word, where there is a distinct upward turn, a longer base line and a small notch at its end. Other features include two clear words, *bn,* and the name '*Ali,* with the tail of the final *yā'* returning to the right to underline the whole word.

Still in the field of inscriptions, though looking much more like the Arabic to which we are used, is a series of texts dating from the first century of Islam/seventh century CE and found within the Arabian Peninsula. Three can be mentioned in some detail. The first is an inscription on a dam near al-Ṭā'if and the so-called Kufic style of writing is beginning to show itself. It is dated 58/677 and is of great importance because of the clear dots which can be seen and which are used to distinguish otherwise identical letters. One can make out the letters *bā*', *tā*', *thā*', *nūn* and *yā*' by the number and position of the dots which are featured almost exactly as we would see them today.

More first/seventh century examples are the two from Mecca dated 80/699. Both contain quotations from the Quran. Despite its obvious epigraphic appearance and its evident square features, it gives the distinct impression of a cursive hand. The two are the work of the same hand and the author was a certain 'Uthmān. The hand has already rid itself of clear Nabataean influence and is to be linked closely with the early Kufic Quran manuscripts which are dealt with in the following chapter.

An important development of the Arabic script during this first century of Islam was its use in a monumental inscription, that of the famous Dome of the Rock in Jerusalem (Illustration 10). The interior and exterior band of inscriptions is inlaid in mosaic, gold on a blue background. The date is given 72/691. The inscription mentions the construction of the mosque and is otherwise a collection of Quranic verses. Interestingly, some of these verses do not tally with the eventual Uthmanic version of the text and there are slight orthographic differences. Of utmost interest is the use of dots to distinguish letters, albeit in an unusual way (e.g. three dots

10. Monumental Inscription, Dome of the Rock, Jerusalem

in a line for one *shīn*, three dots, one above the others for another; two dots one above the other for *tā'*). Also it is clear that this is the forerunner of the monumental Kufic script which played such a huge part as a major architectural feature throughout the centuries after the advent of Islam.

To sum up, we can see that from about the fourth century CE through to the seventh, the first of the Islamic calendar, the Arabic script was developing out of the Nabataean script, and the Arabic inscriptions, all incidentally in the general area of Greater Syria and the northern Arabian Peninsula, take on a script form which we readily recognize from our knowledge of the script today. It was not, however, until the first/seventh century that we see for the first time dots being used to distinguish various letters which would otherwise be identical. Still to come (below) and closely connected with the text of the Quran and its precise understanding are vowel signs, signs which enable the reader to read short vowels and diphthongs correctly.

IV - The Arabic Papyri

Since the third millennium BCE, papyrus has been manufactured in Egypt to provide writing material. The papyrus reed (*Cyperus papyrus*) grows in abundance in the marshy areas of the Nile valley. Strips cut or torn the length of the triangular-shaped stem, set at right angles, are beaten together and the plant's natural juices provide the adhesion necessary for a stable writing surface. While papyrus is perhaps predominantly associated with ancient Egyptian writings, it was also used for the writing of Aramaic (including Nabataean) and there is a considerable corpus of Arabic papyri in different libraries throughout the world and the scripts employed are of relevance to our story.

The earliest extant Arabic papyrus dates from the first/seventh century and through time until the arrival of paper in the Middle East about the fifth/eleventh, the material was used by the literate of Egypt, whether for highly official documents or for the most casual private note. The range was enormous: legal documents, private, official and semi-official letters on many different subjects, money matters, written orders, petitions, casual notes, religious matters; the list is endless.

مالله ا لر حمرا لد حلو فظا ما احد عبدا لله
حدو ا صلة مرا لحد مرا فلبرا خذنا
حلفه دد و ا ارا و مدا لا حصد و مرحكمها / صطعا ام / بو قلا لا حد مهسل ثننا ه
مزا لخذ د و خمس عبد د سا ه ا حد ی / حد د ها ا حمد سعند و حلد و لعلا فی
ننلهد جمد ی لا و لی مرسنه ا علمو عسرو صله ا م حد د د

11. Earliest known Arabic papyrus, dated 22 (643 CE)

The earliest known Arabic papyrus (22/643) (Illustration 11) is of immense historical interest and is a receipt given by the Arab commander in Egypt during the Muslim conquest, 'Abdallāh b. Jābir, for 65 sheep for the provision of his troops. The text itself reveals a rather crude hand to our present-day way of thinking, though much can be made out from even a cursory study of the document. Not surprisingly, the whole document has a generally cursive appearance, although letters like *sīn* and *shīn* are given distinct teeth. Three dots (in a straight line) appear twice over the letter *shīn* and the superscript single dot for *nūn*, the subscript dot for *jīm* and the superscript dot for *khā'*. In addition, the Arabic word *akhadhnā*, "we have taken", has a complete set of diacritics.

Bearing in mind that the Arabic material written on papyrus covers such a vast array of different subjects and would have been written by a range of writers from government clerk to private individual, it is nevertheless possible to detect a development of the script throughout the centuries during which papyrus was in use as a writing material. The discipline of palaeography can and indeed must be applied as much in the case of papyrus as in any other genre of written material in which we are interested. Looking for example at a papyrus of the second/eighth century (Illustration 12), a semi-official

12. Arabic papyrus, 131 (748 CE)

request for the allocation of two post mounts, we note again a rather crude cursive script. There are no diacritical dots to distinguish letters and this serves as a timely reminder that our comments above on the existence of such dots in a first/ seventh century document in no way imply that such dots were by this time common and permanent. In fact, they are used sparingly throughout the period of Arabic papyri. Another interesting feature is the continuous straight stroke to denote the *sīn/shīn*, a feature extremely common in all Arabic handwriting down to the present time.

In short, then, Arabic documents written on papyrus are attested from the first/seventh through to the fourth/eleventh century when paper, introduced from China through Central

Asia, took over as the main writing material. The subject matter is varied and both official and unofficial material is available in quantity. The scripts are cursive, generally speaking with only a sprinkling of diacritics. Other features well known even to this day in Arabic handwriting, such as the single horizontal stroke for *sīn/shīn*, are found.

It is now time to turn to the strictly formal and exquisitely beautiful forms of the Arabic script as they developed over the centuries, in the first place in order to copy the text of Islam's sacred text, the Quran.

V - The Classical Arabic Scripts
– Kufic and *naskhī*

The year 622 of the Christian era marks Muḥammad's migration from Mecca to Medina, called in Arabic the *hijra*, and this is the beginning of the Islamic calendar. His efforts to win over the predominantly mercantile populace of Mecca had resulted in opposition and outright hostility and his migration to the agriculturally-orientated society of Medina was an astute move which eventually brought about the triumph of the new religion. During the years 622 and 10/632 when Muḥammad died, the text of the Quran came into existence, although it is thought that it was only officially established as the text which we now know during the caliphate of 'Uthmān (23-35/644-56). By this time, the Islamic community was no longer a relatively small one within the Arabian Peninsula; it was rather an expanding empire encompassing vast areas of Egypt and North Africa in the west, Greater Syria and Iraq, and Iran and beyond in the east, populated by diverse groups and nations, many of them not native Arabic users. This new Islamic community had to be supplied with an authoritative text and the practice of copying this sacred text thus began and flourished. From earliest times, Islam as a religion seriously frowned upon the representation of the human form, so much a part of Christian iconography, and the highest art form was undoubtedly the written word. With the feverish efforts to copy the text and the ever greater artistic feeling among calligraphers, there developed the two major Arabic scripts: Kufic and *naskhī*, the former seemingly associated with the town in southern Iraq, Kufa, although no precise connection has ever been established, and the latter, the *"copying"* hand. It may be noted that the Nabataean Aramaic word for "copy" is *nishṭā*, from the same root as *naskhī*.

Naturally, the writing material of the scribe to a considerable extent dictated which of the two scripts he employed, and indeed how exactly he formed his handwriting within their general features. Parchment, papyrus and, later, paper would naturally lead to a more cursive style written with a pen, a type of *naskhī*, while lapidary inscriptions, on tombstones, buildings etc., as well as writings on metals, on coins and metalwork for example, are much more likely to steer the scribe into a squarer, more formal style, one of the various forms of Kufic.

Both Kufic and *naskhī* continued over the centuries and the latter is the precursor of modern printed Arabic. Both too found their way in time onto material other than parchment, papyrus or paper; both have been used extensively in architectural works, ceramics, textiles, woodwork and metal-work. We might mention here that Kufic was the norm in early and medieval coinage. It is important, however, to stress that these are not just two scripts, but rather under the heading of each we find a number of different types which are the subject of this chapter. One might perhaps add that there is no general consensus on the naming and description of what sometimes appears as a myriad of sub-divisions of both Kufic and *naskhī*. We have chosen what we consider to be the most important here and have tried to simplify the issue.

We shall begin with Kufic. However, mention should first be made of a very interesting script in which some of the earliest copies of the Quran were made. The script which is associated with several surviving Quranic texts of the first/ seventh century from the Arabian Peninsula is called in Arabic *mā'il*, "slanting" (Illustration 13). Its immediately obvious feature is the slanting uprights of the vertical strokes, most clearly seen in the *alif*s and the *lām*s, which slope to the right at an approximate angle of 45 degrees. It has no diacritics, nor vowel signs. It is an angular script rather than a cursive and must thus be seen as the forerunner of Kufic.

The Kufic Quran has reached its fully developed form by the end of the second/eighth century (Illustration 14). It was invariably written on parchment, the letters in a black ink with dots, often red and green (the latter used with initial *hamza*) though sometimes in gold only, representing short vowels, and black strokes, single and double, distinguishing letters. The text thus written is made difficult by the spacing which would seem to be more to do with the calligrapher's artistic inclinations and his desire to justify his text precisely than with Arabic orthography. "Justification" here refers to what became the standard practice in printed books of making the lines even in length both at the beginning and at the end of

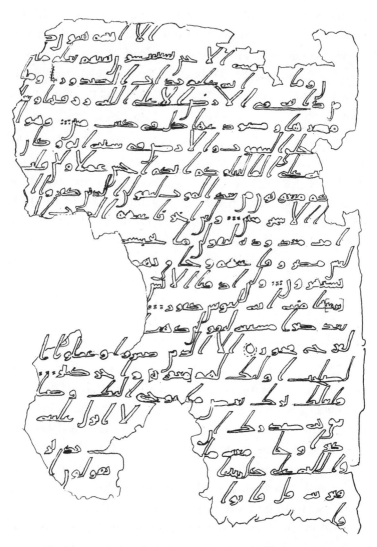

13. Quranic fragment, *mā'il* script, first century of Islam

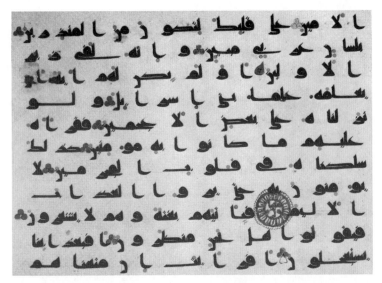

14. Kufic Quran, second/eighth century

the lines. Verse endings and other pauses call for gold: usually a cluster of three balls, one sitting on two others and quite elaborate roundels. Readers should note that final *mīm* now has acquired a tiny tail and final *nūn* does not yet form the semi-circle which we see in the *naskhī* script. Frequently, marginal illuminations can be found in gold and chapter headings too are written in gold. The codices produced for such Kufic Qurans have a horizontal format, the top and bottom of each leaf being longer than the two sides, what in today's computerized printing is called "landscape" as contrasted with "portrait".

From about the late fourth/tenth century, one begins to detect a distinct western development, western Kufic (Illustration 15), with its origins in North Africa and which was to herald

87

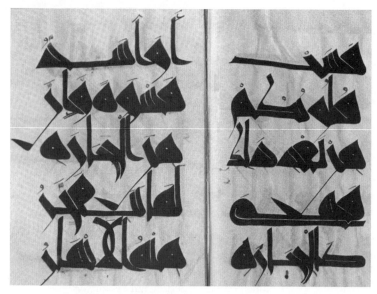

15. Western Kufic Quran, fourth/tenth century

an entirely distinctive Maghrebi script later (see below, Chapter VI). As if in reply at about the same time or a little later, we see an eastern Kufic (Illustration 16), appearing in Iraq and Iran. Both continued to rely on the strong black ink to make the forms of the letters and – in the early stages at any rate – they used coloured dots with gold decorations. The eastern development in particular began to acquire a more familiar appearance, with black dots to distinguish letters and short vowels and other orthographic signs in a form readily recognizable today.

The Kufic story is not quite told, for it is necessary to deal briefly with the script and its development used as a tool in inscriptions, be they lapidary – funerary or architectural – or

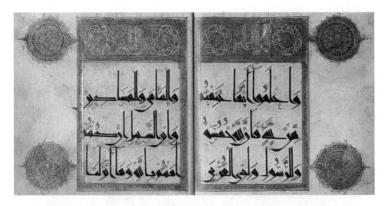

16. Eastern Kufic Quran, Late fourth/tenth century

numismatic. The difficulties of nomenclature have already been mentioned and the epigraphic role of Kufic can perhaps be reduced to three important types. By the fifth/eleventh century, *foliated* Kufic was much in evidence, so called because leaves formed the decoration of the apices of the letters. *Floriated* Kufic has much the same decoration with the addition of floral motifs growing from the terminations of the letters (Illustration 17). The third type is *plaited* Kufic, in which the letter shapes are woven or plaited together to form an elaborate, pleasing and usually entirely symmetrical pattern (Illustration 18).

It is time now to turn to *naskhī* and to remind ourselves that an even greater plethora of different – not to say confusing – technical terms than that mentioned above in the context of Kufic applies also to this script. Once again we must try to clarify and simplify.

It would be wrong to think that *naskhī*, the cursive "copying" script, developed out of Kufic. We can indeed see the

89

17. Floriated Kufic, fifth/eleventh century

18. Plaited Kufic, sixth/twelfth century

beginnings of *naskhī* in the papyrus scripts described above and a relatively quick, cursive hand grew along with the angular Kufic from earliest times. The fact that the formal calligraphic *naskhī* which is extant dates mainly from the seventh/thirteenth century and later certainly does not mean that it is a late form. This form of script is the closest to the earlier Nabataean writing.

We do in fact have an excellent example of a simple *naskhī* Quran manuscript dated 391/1000. Both the calligraphy and the illumination were carried out by the famous Ibn al-Bawwāb (Illustration 19). One can note that all diacritics and vowel and other orthographic signs are provided in exactly the same form as we know them today. The marginal roundels in lapis lazuli and gold and the striking gold headings make for a pleasingly simple, if somewhat crowded, overall effect. It is possible to see catchwords at the bottom left of the verso of the folio. However, this should not be taken as contemporary with the copying of the manuscript and has clearly been added at a later date.

The technical terms associated with the cursive *naskhī* script are many and apt to confuse. The confusion is compounded by the fact that the term *naskhī*, as well as denoting the cursive genre as a whole, is used for a sub-division of it! The Abbasid vizier, Ibn Muqla (d. 330/940), is the first name to appear in connection with the teaching of the rules of cursive writing. Ibn al-Nadīm, the author of the famous *Fihrist* (compiled c. 377/987), mentions twelve main scripts and a further twelve variations! Here we shall go along with Ibn Muqla who is famed for the six categories of *naskhī* which he lists and describes: *thulth, naskh, rayḥān, muḥaqqaq, tawqī*ʿ

91

19. Ibn Al-Bawwāb, Naskhī Quran, 391/1000 CE

and *riqā'* (singular: *ruq'a*). Muslim calligraphers regard *thulth* ("third", perhaps so called because a third of each letter inclines) as the "mother" of this cursive group and *naskhī* as the normal writing and later printing script (Illustration 20). *Muḥaqqaq* is principally characterized by the angle of the left corner of certain letters like *bā'*, *tā'*, *thā'*, *dāl*, *dhāl* etc. *Rayḥān* is a version of *muḥaqqaq*, but differs in that its letters have sharp ends (Illustration 21). *Tawqī'* is a heavier

20. Thulth (above) and Naskhī Quran

21. Muḥaqqaq (above) and Rayḥān (below)

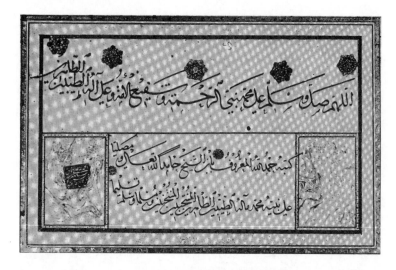

22. Riqāʿ (below)

chancellery script with long sweeps between letters and *sīn/ shīn* already appearing as a horizontal stroke. *Riqāʿ* has survived to be adapted as a very quick handwriting style to this day (see Chapter VII) (Illustration 22).

VI - The Arabic Scripts beyond the Arab Heartlands – North Africa, Iran and Turkey

The Muslim conquests begun in the first/seventh century spread the message of Islam far and wide. The whole of North Africa became part of the Islamic world. In the late first/early eighth century, a member of the Umayyad family fled to the Iberian peninsula from the increasingly powerful Abbasids in the east. Muslim rule over Spain was to last there until the ninth/fifteenth century. For more than seven hundred years, therefore, Spain was an important part of the Islamic world. Similar Muslim expansion took place from earliest Islamic times in the east, and Iraq, Iran and Central Asia and much of the north of the Indian sub-continent, as well as Turkey under the Ottoman sultans, became Islamic in religion and culture. The Arabic alphabet spread too and it is not surprising over such a vast area of the globe that different regions of the Islamic world produced their own particular styles of the Arabic script. Some of the most important of North Africa, Iran and Turkey are the subject of this chapter.

Let us turn to North Africa and Spain first. The Maghrebi script is the name given to that which predominated in the whole of the area. It is the one cursive script which developed directly out of the Kufic which we have discussed above. The earlier history of the Maghrebi script is something of a mystery, for our prime examples date from the sixth/twelfth century. It should be noted too that parchment continued to be used as a writing material much later in the west than in the east which had begun to use paper from about the fourth/tenth century. A wonderful example of Maghrebi is shown in Illustration 23. Its Kufic origins are immediately obvious. Vowel and other orthographic signs are in a light blue ink in contrast to the gold of the actual letters. Some diacritics unique to the Maghrebi script (which indeed continue to this day in North

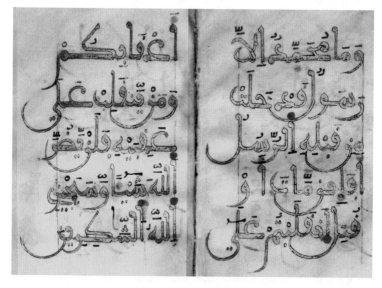

23. Maghrebi, sixth/twelfth century

Africa) should be noted. The *qāf* has only one dot above the letter (line 2), while the letter *fā'* carries its dot *underneath* (line 3). The shapes of some letters are of some interest too. In the *lām-alif* the tail of the former swings right round in a semi-circle, almost returning to touch the *alif*. The flat base of the *'ayn* recalls the Kufic, as does the long, horizontal base of the *kāf* with its parallel second stroke.

Both Iran and Turkey have over the centuries been important centres of Arabic calligraphy, that is displayed in the superb codices of Islam and in the equally fine architecture. For the most part in both countries, the classical Kufic and *naskhī* scripts described above were employed in their manuscript and architectural works of art. In the late seventh/thirteenth century the centre of calligraphic gravity shifted eastwards from the Baghdad of the Abbasids to eastern centres like Herat, Mashhad, Tabriz and Tehran. The "canonical" six scripts described above were further developed and two important scripts added: *ta'līq* and *nasta'līq*, both also occurring in their *shikasta* ("broken") form. *Ta'līq* ("suspension") takes its name from the fact that its letters are joined together with words running into each other (Illustration 24). This quick hand with diacritics often missing and *sīn/shīn* written as a line without teeth was used from the fifth/eleventh or sixth/twelfth century in books, but also in official government documents. By the eighth/fourteenth century, it was yielding place to the *shikasta* version. *Nasta'līq* (Illustration 25) was supposedly a combination of *ta'līq* and *naskhī*. It certainly appears a much more formal hand than *ta'līq* and goes back probably to the seventh/thirteenth century. What was to develop into the *shikasta*

24. Ta'līq

25. Nasta'līq

26. Shikasta

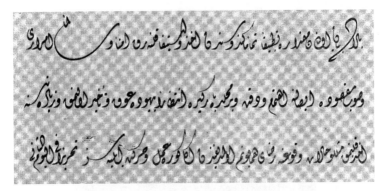

27. Dīwānī

script appeared in the eleventh/seventeenth century. It is a very fine, sweeping script, extremely difficult to read, and is particularly associated with literary works, especially poetry (Illustration 26).

What of Turkey, another important centre of Arabic calligraphy? The Turks too followed the "canonical six" scripts down to the conquest of Constantinople in 857/1453. Istanbul was little by little to become a major centre of the art of calligraphy. The Turks made full use of the classical scripts which have all received attention above. The important addition, the *diwānī* (Illustration 27), is said to have been invented for the diwans created by Mehmed II after the conquest of Constantinople. Attractive to the eye, though difficult to read without a thorough knowledge of the script, *diwānī* has much in common with *riqāʿ* which in a sense is a simplified form of it. One final major calligraphic development closely associated with Turkey is the *ṭughrā*, in which calligraphy is used and moulded to form the picture of an object, a ship, a bird etc., or any pleasing shape

101

28. Ottoman Ṭughrā

(Illustration 28). Different Ottoman sultans adopted their own personalized *ṭughrā*s which were used on official correspondence and documents.

VII - Arabic Writing Today

The Arabic alphabet is alive and well and can be commonly found in all Muslim countries throughout the world. Arabic is the official language of twenty-three countries in Africa and the Middle East with a combined population of approximately 325 millions. In addition, approximately one and one half billion people, about one fifth of the world's population, are Muslims who read and actively use the script, at least for the purpose of worship.

A number of languages, totally unrelated to Arabic, yet whose speakers are Muslims, still to this day use the Arabic script. The major example is Persian, an Indo-European language, which from the early days of Islam in the first/seventh century took over the Arabic alphabet, along with many Arabic words, for its own use. A number of Arabic letters are superfluous in Persian, except for Arabic loan words (e.g. the so-called emphatics), and a number were added on, being lacking in Arabic (e.g. /p/, /ch/ etc.). Pashto, the major language of Afghanistan and of many people in Pakistan, also makes use of the Arabic alphabet. We must also mention

Urdu in this context, the official language of Pakistan and the everyday language of millions in India. Urdu generally uses a form of *nastaʿlīq* (see Chapter VI) and employs also the additional letters required by the language found in the Persian alphabet. Finally, we note that the Somali language is also written in the Arabic script.

Yet a further group of languages (once again all of them Muslim in religion and culture) has used the Arabic alphabet in the past, but has now changed to Roman. Turkish is the obvious example. Since at least the eighth/fourteenth century when it came into being, the Ottoman state employed the Arabic alphabet for Ottoman Turkish. In 1928, Kemal Atatürk as part of his modernization policy for Turkey decreed that Turkish would use the Roman alphabet with some adaptations (for example, *ç* for /ch/, *ş* for /sh/, the dotless *ı* and the *c* used for the sound /j/). This is the practice to this day. Other languages have now abandoned the Arabic alphabet. The major west African language, Hausa, was traditionally written in an Arabic script called *ajami* (from the Arabic "foreign"). A Roman alphabet was introduced under British rule in Nigeria and in 1930 the so-called *boko* (from the English "book") became the official alphabet. From the eighth/fourteenth century, Malay was written in the Arabic alphabet in Malaya and Indonesia. British and Dutch colonial rule encouraged a change to Roman. As for Swahili, the major language of east Africa, from the eighteenth century the first written examples of the language were produced in the Arabic alphabet. Under colonial pressure in the nineteenth century, the language changed to the Roman alphabet.

The Arabic scripts in their classical forms are still used widely in many forms of artistic decoration: in modern art, in architecture etc., for example, where superb calligraphic work can still be found. Modern art in the Arab world has become Europeanized in the twentieth and twenty-first centuries, but it is remarkable that the Arabic alphabet, as if recalling past calligraphic glories, often finds a place there. Not surprisingly, it was *naskhī* that was eventually to provide a printing script in the modern Arab world; well-printed newspapers, magazines and books are written in a neat, pleasing *naskhī* script, although other scripts are employed too for headlines or headings in general. All printed Arabic, with the exception of Quranic texts which are fully vocalized, appear entirely bereft of vowel and orthographic signs, unless of course there is some linguistic ambiguity. Naturally, printed poetry will show many more signs than prose texts. It perhaps goes without saying that all diacritics, the dots used to distinguish identical letters, are standard in printed Arabic.

It is difficult to be precise about dates, but the system of employing dots to distinguish otherwise identical letters must have begun in the first/seventh century. Vowel and other orthographic markers too must be of early use. Such is the nature of Arabic manuscript writing, right through the medieval period to the nineteenth century in which dots and vowel markers were very frequently ignored, that any attempt at dating the finalization of the use of dots would be rash. The dots, the short vowel markers and other signs such as the *sukūn* ("resting"), a small circle included to indicate that the letter concerned is followed by no vowel at all, and *shadda* ("strengthening"), a small *sīn* in appearance and actually a *shīn*, to indicate that the letter concerned is doubled, were in all probability only standardized with the advent of Arabic printing. The latter appears first in the tenth/

sixteenth century in Europe and in the Middle East from the seventeenth.

Arabic printing has undergone a tremendous transformation in recent years with the advent of computers. The relevant software can sort out which form of a letter is required and it does this by recognizing what went before and what comes after. It instantly corrects itself so that the correct combination appears on screen and in print.

Arabic handwriting, in common indeed with that in other scripts, has become more and more difficult to read, taking short cuts to achieve speed and convenience. It certainly is the development of the *riqā'* script described above. The teeth of letters disappear where possible (e.g. *sīn/shīn*) and the letters are merely horizontal strokes. More than one dot is written as a continuous stroke, two dots a short line above (*tā'*) or below the letter form (*yā'*). Above the letter *thā'*, the three dots are written above as a small circumflex accent. Final *nūn* and *qāf* tend to lose their dots and, as if in compensation, end with a flourishing tail rather than with a neat semi-circle.

Out of the first century CE Nabataean consonantal alphabet and having added vowel signs and diacritics under the influence of Syriac in the first/seventh century, the Arabic alphabet today serves millions, native speakers and non-Arab Muslims alike.

Illustration Sources

1. Brooklyn Museum
2. Welles et al., *Parchments and Papyri* (1959), plate LXIX, Yale University Press
3. John Healey
4. John Healey
5. Ada Yardeni, Israel Exploration Society
6. John Healey
7. © British Library Board. All Rights Reserved. Add. 12150, f.200
8. Ecole Biblique, Jerusalem
9. E.J. Brill
10. Beatrice Gruendler
11. E.J. Brill
12. John Rylands University Library, Special Collections
13. © Biblioteca Apostolica Vaticana (Vatican)
14. © British Library Board, All Rights Reserved. Or.139, f., 15v
15. Ibrahim ibn al-Aghlab Museum

16. Mashhad Shrine Library
17. © bpk / Museum für Islamische Kunst, Staatliche Museen zu Berlin. Photo: Georg Niedermeiser
18. Sircali Medresse, Konya, Turkey
19. © The Trustees of the Chester Beatty Library, Dublin
20. Topkapi Palace Museum
21. Topkapi Palace Museum
22. Topkapi Palace Museum
23. John Rylands University Library, Special Collections
24. Topkapi Palace Museum
25. Topkapi Palace Museum
26. Fogg Art Museum, Harvard University
27. Izzet Effendi
28. Sabahettin Uzluk, *Mevlevilikte Resim, Resimde Mevleviler*, Ankara 1957

Further Reading

Abbott, N. *The Rise of the North Arabic Script and its Kur'anic Development.* Chicago 1939.

Arif, Aida S. *Arabic Lapidary Kufic in Africa. Egypt, North Africa, Sudan. A Study of the Development of the Kufic Script (3rd–6th Century AH/9th–12th Century AD).* London 1967.

Dalby, Andrew. *Dictionary of Languages.* London 1998.

Diringer, David. *The Alphabet: a Key to the History of Mankind.* London 1968 (3rd ed.).

Driver, G. R. *Semitic Writing from Pictograph to Alphabet.* London 1976 (3rd ed.).

Encyclopaedia of Islam. Second Edition. "Khaṭṭ".

Gacek, Adam. *The Arabic Manuscript Tradition. A Glossary of Technical Terms and Bibliography.* Leiden, Boston and Cologne 2001.

Grohmann, Adolf. *From the World of Arabic Papyri.* Cairo 1952.

Grohmann, Adolf. *Arabische Paläographie.* 2 vols. Vienna 1967, 1971.

Gruendler, Beatrice. *The Development of the Arabic Scripts.*

From the Nabatean Era to the First Century according to Dated Texts. Atlanta 1993.

Hanebutt-Benz, E., Glass, D. and Roper, G. (eds in collaboration with Th. Smets). *Middle Eastern Languages and the Print Revolution: a Cross-cultural Encounter*. Westhofen 2002.

Healey, John F. *The Early Alphabet*. London 1990.

Healey, John F. "The Early History of the Syriac Script: a reassessment". *Journal of Semitic Studies* 45 (2000), 55-67.

Healey, John and Smith, G. Rex. "Jaussen-Savignac 17 – the Earliest Dated Arabic Document". *Atlal* 12 (1989), 77-84.

Lings, Martin. *The Quranic Art of Calligraphy and Illumination*. London 1976.

Mitshu, Kawatuku. *Mash athari fī junūb wa-gharb al-Mamlaka al-ʿArabiyya al-Suʿūdiyya 1422/2002. Atlal* 18 (1426/2005), 141-52.

al-Muaikel, Khaleel. "Pre-Islamic Inscriptions from Sakaka, Saudi Arabia" in J.F. Healey and V. Porter (eds), *Studies on Arabia in Honour of Professor G. Rex Smith*. Oxford 2002, 157-71.

Naveh, Joseph. *The Development of the Aramaic Script*. Jerusalem 1970.

Naveh, Joseph. *Early History of the Alphabet: an Introduction to West Semitic Epigraphy and Palaeography*. Jerusalem/Leiden 1982.

Pattie, T. S. and Turner, E. G. *The Written Word on Papyrus*. London 1974.

Safadi, Y.H. *Islamic Calligraphy*. London 1978.

Schimmel, Annemarie. *Islamic Calligraphy*. Leiden 1970.

Smith, G. Rex and al-Moraekhi, Moshalleh. *The Arabic Papyri of the John Rylands University Library of Manchester*.

Bulletin of the John Rylands University Library of Manchester 78/2 (1996).

al-Thuniyān, Muḥammad b. ʿAbd al-Raḥmān. *Ḥaṣr wa-tawthīq al-kitābāt al-ṣakhriyya al-islāmiyya al-muʾarrakha al-muktashifa ʿalā arāḍī al-Mamlaka al-ʿArabiyya al-Suʿūdiyya.* Forthcoming.*

* The authors wish to thank Dr al-Thenayian for his help in dealing with the early Arabic inscriptions.

INDEX

Page numbers in *italic* refer to illustrations.